FOREWORD BY
laura robb

MIDDLE
SCHOOL
READERS

HELPING THEM READ WIDELY,

HELPING THEM READ WELL

NANCY ALLISON

heinemann
portsmouth, nh

To my father

Heinemann
361 Hanover Street
Portsmouth, NH 03801–3912
www.heinemann.com

Offices and agents throughout the world

© 2009 by Nancy Allison

Library of Congress Cataloging-in-Publication Data
Allison, Nancy.
   Middle school readers : helping them read widely, helping them read well / Nancy Allison ; foreword by Laura Robb
      p. cm.
   Includes bibliographical references.
   ISBN-13: 978-0-325-02814-9
   ISBN-10: 0-325-02814-1
   1. Reading (Middle school).   2. Motivation in education.   I. Title.

LB1632.A57 2009
428.4071'2—dc22   2009017081

Editor: Wendy Murray
Production: Vicki Kasabian
Cover design: Jenny Jensen Greenleaf
Cover and interior photographs: Andrew Robia
Typesetter: Aptara,® Inc.
Manufacturing: Valerie Cooper

Printed in the United States of America on acid-free paper
13   12   VP   3   4   5

CONTENTS

Foreword by Laura Robb vi

Acknowledgments viii

1 The Teacher on the Sidelines of Independent Reading 1
    A Call to Change   2
    Parting Ways with the Whole-Class Novel   3
    Choice: A Critical Factor in Engagement   5
    Texts That Spur Growth   6
    How Not to Squander Independent Reading Time   6
    Handing Over Responsibility to Students   7
    Dovetailing Independent Reading in the Balanced Literacy Classroom   8
    The Difference a Change Can Make   11
    Questions for Reflection   12

**2 Planning for Engagement: Coloring and Contouring
Students' Expectations** 13
    Students' Prior Experiences   14
    Shaping Students' Concept of Reader   15
    Do All Readers Lug Heavy Tote Bags? Modeling the Behavior of a Reader   15
    Windows on Their World: Reading Autobiographies   17
    Inviting Students into the Reader's World   20
    Book Talks: Plot Teaser Moments That Motivate   20
    Daily Exchanges: Sustaining Engagement, Confirming Membership   22
    Engaging Students Through Small-Group Sharing   23
    The Difference Engagement Can Make   25
    Questions for Reflection   26

3 Clever Matchmaking Between Students and Books 27
    Building a Robust Classroom Library   28
    Making the Classroom Library Accessible   30
    Planning for Student Choice   35
    Creating Excitement About Fiction   36
    Launch a Shopping Spree for a Perfect Match   38
    Book Talking Nonfiction   42
    Book Shopping Record Sheets: Early in the Year Assessment Tools   44
    The Benefit of Time Well Spent   49
    Making Good Choices in the Library   49

    Teaching a Reader's Expectations for Books   50
    Easing the Hunt for Books   51
    Questions for Reflection   55

4 Direct Instruction and Routines in the Independent Reading Classroom **57**
    Teaching Through Minilessons   58
    Breaking Down a Complex Task: Three Types of Knowledge   58
    Anchoring the Lesson in Common Texts   59
    Using Anchor Charts to Hold Shared Thinking   60
    Anchor Charts in Action: Lesson on Inferences   61
    Reading Responses That Link Instruction and Practice   64
    Teaching the Routine of Supported Independent Reading Time   65
    The Difference Seamless Instruction Can Make   67
    Questions for Reflection   67

5 Teaching Through Deskside Conferences **69**
    Deskside Conferences as Vehicles for Teaching   70
    The Purpose and Structure of a Conference   71
    Preparing for the Conference   72
    Initiating the Conference   73
    Focusing the Conference   74
    Checking for Understanding   76
    Keeping a Record of Deskside Conferences   76
    The Difference a Conference Can Make   80
    Questions for Reflection   82

6 Capturing the Attention of Our Disengaged Readers **83**
    Dealing with "Boring" Texts: The Abandonment Conference   84
    Understanding What Keeps Readers Reading   86
    Dealing with Distractions   88
    Assessing the Comprehension of Disengaged Students   93
    Using Questions to Engage Readers   96
    Questioning the Author's Intent   100
    Questions as a Response to Engage Readers   101
    A Conference Focused on Questioning   102
    Questions for Reflection   106

7 Differentiating Instruction Through Deskside Conferences **107**
    Today's Reality   108
    Differentiating Instruction for Independent Readers   109
    Delayed Readers   110
    On-Level Readers   115
    Gifted Readers   119
    The Rewards of Supporting Independent Readers   121
    Questions for Reflection   123

8 Teaching Comprehension in Fiction Texts **124**
    Redirecting Growing Readers   125
    Story Structure: The Basis of Questions About Fiction   127

    Detecting Point of View *137*
    Supporting Readers of Fiction *141*
    Questions for Reflection *142*

9 Teaching Comprehension in Nonfiction Texts **143**
    Bridging to Informational Texts *144*
    Understanding the Purpose of Nonfiction Texts *145*
    The Power of Pictures *146*
    Reading Informational Texts *147*
    Nonfiction Conferences *148*
    The True Meaning of K-W-L *149*
    Expecting New Learning *151*
    Deepening Knowledge: The Basis of Questions About Nonfiction *152*
    Broadening the Vision of Reading *153*
    Questions for Reflection *153*

10 Assessing Independent Readers **154**
    Reading Response *155*
    Assessing Reading Responses *158*
    Reading Log *161*
    Assessing Reading Logs *163*
    Final Thoughts: The Power of Change *164*

Study Guide **165**

References **177**

FOREWORD

When I finished *Middle School Readers* I wanted to reverse time and relive sixth grade as a student in Nancy Allison's class. For me, sixth-grade reading was one anthology for everyone, dozens of worksheets to complete each week, and unit tests that had nothing to do with the stories we read. I remember I failed a reading test on making inferences. I didn't know what an inference was, so I checked all the statements under the paragraph. Most of the class failed. I can still picture our teacher's angry face as she blamed us, insisting we failed because we didn't listen, didn't read directions, didn't care. As an adult I can understand the teacher's frustration but I still smart at the unleashing of blame on us, and how she could only see as far as what we couldn't do. We hadn't failed the test, we'd failed her.

That event could never happen in Nancy Allison's class. Allison's empathy for her students, coupled with a deep and inspiring knowledge of how to teach reading, supports every student's growth whether they are developing, reluctant, grade-level, or proficient readers.

If you aspire to improve the reading skill of every student you teach, if you dream of a personal reading life for all middle school learners who step over the threshold of your classroom, and if you recognize that all students, even those who appear to be disengaged from reading want to read, then let Nancy Allison be your personal guide, your beacon, as you help students make sense of our complex world and lives through reading.

Weaving literacy stories of conferences with dozens of students into lessons that differentiate reading and offer students choice, Allison takes us into her own unique brand of reading workshop. There she shows the benefits of moving from one novel, one basal, one teacher choosing the books students read to inviting students to choose books on topics they care and are passionate about because reading such books helps every student move forward. With thought and clarity, and with honesty and a deep sensitivity to providing the finest road map for teachers, Allison provides research-based ways to support students' book selection and to establish class routines. She also builds students' mental models of reading with read-alouds, which make visible to students how she works hard to comprehend the fiction and nonfiction anchor texts she shares.

We meet a diverse group of readers and come to understand the power of daily deskside conferences that honor each reader but also enable them to build skill and stamina with books they choose at their instructional reading level. Allison models how she supports disengaged readers with powerful questions that encourage these students to think carefully about their reading, to see and feel their progress. Allison's teaching sense and know-how, her nurturing and gentle nudging to try again and work hard to construct meaning from reading comes across with every conference and sends the message that we must never give up on a student, even if that student appears to have given up on herself.

Ultimately, what Allison communicates to teachers is that to help students read fiction and nonfiction, to refine their knowledge of genre structure and reading strategies, we must engage in conversations with students that lead them to independence. Allison reminds us that independence isn't something instantly bestowed on middle schoolers but something they both learn and earn. That is, they have to develop and cultivate the skills needed to solve their own reading problems as they take on more challenging texts. And teachers are on the sidelines of this transformation, coaching, clarifying, cheerleading.

Allison invites teachers to show students how to shop for or choose "just-right books" and what to do if students' choices don't work. Her literacy stories celebrate and emphasize the importance of choice. Like many of us, she's done the one-book-for-all and the teacher-chosen books for students. However, if we are to improve the reading expertise of every student in our classes, then, like Allison, we must abandon what doesn't work and meet our students' diverse needs by differentiating reading instruction and using conferences to engage them with their reading.

The rich and detailed accounts that Nancy Allison shares in this book show teachers how to help students approach new genres, how to make inferences and connections, what to do when a text confuses a reader, and how to asses through reading response and reading logs. She leaves readers lingering over the idea that it's we teachers who can and do make a difference in students' reading lives. And that teaching reading is about learning from our students, helping them find joy in reading books they select, and watching them grow personal reading lives that can feed their emotional and intellectual selves and at the same time prepare them for the demands of high school, college, and the workplace.

Laura Robb

ACKNOWLEDGMENTS

This book has been a long journey that would never have been possible without the guidance of two outstanding educators, Dr. Judy Wallis and Dr. Lee Mountain. Judy has taught me everything I know about reading and has always encouraged me to try new things and to explore new thoughts. She is never too busy to listen and always knows in exactly what direction to point me, including toward Heinemann. She has truly changed my life.

Dr. Mountain is a blessing to every life she touches. Her belief in her students and their ability to have something worthwhile to say has inspired countless educators to put words to paper. Her unfailing belief in me matters.

If I'm ever again caught in a whirlwind, I know who I want to be there with me: Kerry Herlihy and my husband, Harry. Thanks to both of you for helping me survive two frantic weeks in March. And thanks to my daughters and grandchildren who understood when I didn't answer the phone.

Very sincere thanks go to Wendy Murray for her exceptional ideas and guidance and her belief in both me and this book.

Special thanks to Eric Lipper for paving the way for this book to be published.

Perhaps my greatest thanks go to my colleagues at Spring Woods Middle School. Thank you for taking a chance on a person you didn't even know—and being willing to try something new because you wanted the best for your students. I learn from each of you every day and feel truly blessed to work with such student-centered professionals.

Very special and heartfelt thanks go in particular to Cynthia Chai, the principal who believed. Your support of literacy and your heart for children have made a difference in our students' lives and in mine. Thank you.

The Teacher on the Sidelines of Independent Reading

I first met Roderick when he was in the fifth grade. His teacher was out on maternity leave, and I was administering the year-end reading assessment for the long-term substitute. He had already failed our state's reading test twice and was going to be retained in fifth grade if he failed it again after summer school.

To say Roderick was a disengaged reader would be a mild understatement. He was quick to admit he hadn't read a book that year. He scored at the beginning third-grade level on the assessment—nearly three years below grade level—and his third failure of the state test that summer meant he would repeat fifth grade.

Roderick was placed on a fifth-grade intervention team with which I worked the next year. To his credit, he was never oppositional—just disengaged and very delayed in his reading development.

I met with him daily in the fall, conferring with him while he attempted to work his way through texts that would put one small piece of the reading puzzle at a time under his control. It was late October before I saw any signs of change, but then the turnaround was dramatic. One day it struck me that Roderick was suddenly eager to read and seemed lost in his book for the entire reading time.

By November, he was asking his mother to take him to bookstores on the weekends and coming in on Mondays with stacks of books he was now proud to own. Not all of them were good choices for his reading level, but he was suddenly motivated to have books of his own to read. By December he was choosing wisely and reading books on grade level. In March he passed the state reading test with flying colors, a feat no one would have believed possible earlier in the year—and he continued to read, finishing several more books before school dismissed for the summer. At the end of the year, he thanked both his classroom teacher and me, saying that no one had ever taught him as much as we had.

No one had ever taught him as much as we had is a comment that resonates with me to this day—and one that raises a key question for all teachers of reading. What does it mean to "teach" reading in the intermediate grades and middle school? Do we ever teach too little? When are we teaching too much? When do our teaching methods actually impede a student's personal journey to independent, enthusiastic reading?

I know the instruction we provided Roderick that year built on the work others had done before us. Much of what was covered in direct instruction was merely a review of things he had previously been taught both in whole-group and small-group sessions. The biggest difference for Roderick was that the frequent deskside conferences he had with me in the classroom met him at his own point of confusion and gave him the tools he needed to help him grow. The missing piece in his previous instruction had been *supported* independent reading.

This book, then, focuses on exploring ideas for reforming our practices so that students' independent reading becomes the instructional tool we use to help readers grow.

A Call to Change

Three years ago I left a district where I had taught for eighteen years when trade books were replaced with basal readers and independent reading time was relegated to the hallways during breaks in an ill-conceived quest for higher test scores. Forcing students to read excerpts from texts that were not at their appropriate reading levels and did not relate to their life experiences proved to be about as engaging for them as watching grass grow. Even worse, independent student reading decreased from fifty to 100 pages a week to about ten, and students' chance to build stamina by reading in connected text disappeared completely. I could not be a party to what I saw as educational malpractice.

I do not share this story to indict these teaching practices. I taught this way, too, for many years. It worked for some of my students, but certainly not for all. And the students who most needed my help were the ones it consistently failed. Instead I share this story to illustrate that we can't afford to let any portion of our class coast or fail because a test-driven culture has taken hold of our schools.

We now live in a society where students have few reading role models and many competing interests and types of texts beyond the printed page. Many students will not discover the power of reading to teach them about the world and their place in it if they do not discover that power in school. They need language arts classrooms where the shelves are filled with engaging fiction and nonfiction texts—and where their teacher's main responsibility is to support their growth as readers. They deserve to be respected and supported as they work their way through self-selected texts.

This book is at once an urgent call to action and a how-to book for inspiring and supporting even the most reluctant readers in your room. It calls on you to keep independent reading at the center of your teaching, and to articulate to colleagues why it's worth it. It also asks you to look at your practice and be candid with yourself about what's working with independent reading and what's not, and then to use this book to help strengthen every facet of your independent reading program. The change may require a leap of faith, but it will undoubtedly help your students soar.

Parting Ways with the Whole-Class Novel

In the summer of 2006, I spent a day in the literacy center of the middle school where I had just been hired as the language arts specialist. I wanted to be familiar with the resources so I could make informed decisions with the next budget and help teachers find materials.

To my amazement, there were 50–150 copies of almost every book in the room. The large numbers indicated that it was customary for all students to read the same book at the same time under the pacing and direction of their teacher. And in the library, carefully organized, were CDs and tapes of these very same books that the teachers could check out and use with their classes. Students could move from recorded book to recorded book throughout the year and never be held responsible for actually reading the text the class was studying.

Not surprisingly, at the beginning of the year when I asked my grade-level teams what they were teaching the next few weeks, they would answer with titles—"We're teaching *Esperanza Rising* or *The Outsiders*." There was no mention of instructional goals for reading or thinking. The problem was they were teaching books, not readers.

Whole-class novels, often chosen with the best of intentions, do not take reading and interest levels into account. There is no one book that will speak to the needs of every student in my class, and the large block of time usually devoted to these books does not mimic the type of reading real readers do. The time I have with my students is too valuable to waste on practices that don't push them to grow.

More and more often classrooms include below-level readers who are not yet competent enough to comprehend grade-level texts. The whole-group text may be well above even their instructional reading level, and requiring them to read it will not guarantee that they *can*. It is important for me to remember that time spent studying texts above students' reading levels is time lost in developing these students as readers (Allington 2001).

In *How Reading Changed My Life*, Anna Quindlen warns that "one of the most pernicious phenomena in assigned reading is the force-feeding of serious work at an age when the reader will feel pushed away, not from the particular book being assigned, but from an entire class of books, or even books in general" (1998, 55). I cannot afford to employ instructional practices that will drive readers away from rather than toward reading. As a reading teacher, I have come to understand that my teaching should start with the needs of my students, not with a text. No harm will come to students if they do not read *The Outsiders*—but there is a potential for great harm if they don't learn how to infer from clues in the text. Instead of beginning my planning with a book I want them to read, I now begin with the skills or strategies I want my students to master (see Chapter 4) and then choose an engaging text for modeling that lends itself to their application.

Another sometimes-ignored result of teaching one book to the whole class is that it often limits the amount of reading individual students do (Allington 2001). Teachers move at a pace that fits their teaching and usually plan to teach one novel per grading period. Since they devote all their class time to the reading and/or discussion of the chosen book, any reading in self-selected texts is done as homework, if at all. Students who have not yet learned that reading is a pleasant pastime will read only the class novel—and many of them will not actually read that because it is above their reading level and the ensuing class discussions will give them enough knowledge of the text to fake their way through. So just as they've done through much of their academic careers, the students who most need to read will be reading the least—and their attitudes about reading are unlikely to change.

Students will often resist even the best teacher-assigned texts, craving instead the freedom to choose their own texts for their own purposes (Reeves 2004). The students Reeves surveyed repeatedly classed the books their teachers had assigned, no matter how potentially engaging, as boring and admitted they hadn't actually read them. Some had skimmed them, and others had relied on classroom discussion to give them enough information about the book to pass the test.

My conversations with students confirm Reeves' findings. Students often tell me they read *no* books their previous year in school, even if their teachers varied the texts through book clubs. The books were still chosen by someone else, and the classroom activities surrounding those books made it easy for below-level and reluctant readers to hide the truth that they were not reading.

It was hard to give up teaching books I desperately loved. Abandoning projects I'd spent years developing tore at my heart. But if this is the price I must pay to ensure that every student in my room reads a book that is right for him or her, isn't that a terribly small price to pay? I can still recommend those tried and true favorites and use them for book talks and minilessons. And students will still read them—only now they will have chosen them for themselves.

Choice: A Critical Factor in Engagement

If the goal of instruction is to arm students with the skills they need to be proficient independent readers who are committed to a lifetime of reading, then students must be allowed to choose their own books. That is what real readers do. Daniels and Bizar (2005) list student choice as one of the important characteristics of "best practice" classrooms, and student choice has continually been shown to increase intrinsic motivation in learners (Guthrie and Knowles 2001).

Because reluctant readers are just that—reluctant—it is easier to place a book in their hands and require its reading than it is to teach them to find the books on their own. I have put these students in guided reading groups where I chose the book; I also have put them in literature study groups where I either directly chose the book or narrowed the choice to three or four titles deemed to be appropriate, usually based on reading level. I did let students choose their own books in the library—but the students were reading these all on their own and not being held accountable for the reading. Usually these books went into tote trays, backpacks, or lockers for two weeks and were then turned in to be replaced by other books that would meet the same fate. Even though my intentions were good, I was failing reluctant readers again and again.

Students will not continue to grow as readers or find joy in texts if they continually avoid reading. I need to create a classroom culture that invites students to explore a wide variety of texts that will inspire them to think, reexamine their lives, and stretch their minds.

The idea of allowing every student in the room to read a different book was initially overwhelming. So many questions came to mind: What if I haven't read the book? How can I make sure they've understood my curriculum? How can they talk to each other about books if they're all reading something different? What will my principal say? Change always means taking a risk. I believed this change would make a significant difference in the reading lives of my students, and I was right.

Texts That Spur Growth

A commitment to student choice must be coupled with a commitment to teaching students to choose texts that will further their growth as readers. This is not always easy to do. Many students who have continual struggles with reading are very reluctant to leave the comfort of picture books and move into chapter books. Although more and more picture books are being written at higher reading levels and address more sophisticated themes and topics, when students only read texts that can be finished in one sitting they do not build the stamina needed to tackle more advanced, longer texts. These books also do not help students learn to carry information across one chapter to the next or to sustain their interest in the problem and its solution. It would be easier to continue to supply short texts to these students; their reading of these books would require very little intervention. But the time these students spent on these short texts would not accelerate their growth as readers.

Older students sometimes cling to the familiarity of series books rather than making the transition to more sophisticated texts with characters who are older and whose problems more closely mirror their own. Without support from a skilled reader who can guide them through their first experience with these more complicated texts, these readers may not make the transition to age-appropriate reading. If students are to grow as readers, they must be reading texts at increasingly higher levels of difficulty.

Supported independent reading works best when students read in texts at levels that provide enough challenge to be interesting and enough familiarity to be manageable. Students who continually read at a level that presents no challenges for them will make no more gains than students who spend the same amount of time doing activities other than reading (Carver 2000). If students are to thrive as readers, they cannot afford thirty minutes each day of wasted time.

How Not to Squander Independent Reading Time

As an instructional tool, independent reading seldom reaches its full potential. In most classrooms, it is viewed either as a time for the teacher to read along with the students as a model of reading (the sustained silent reading model, or SSR) or as an activity to keep students busy while the teacher works with a small guided reading group. To the teacher devoted to SSR, independent reading is reading done for pleasure during the school day for which students are not held accountable in any way. To the teacher who guides small groups during this time, independent reading is often time set aside for students to read in books that require no teacher intervention, reading logs, or responses. Both of these models diminish independent reading time's connection to instruction.

Instruction implies that someone—namely, the teacher—is actually helping the learner learn. According to Vygotsky (1978), student growth occurs when instruction is given in what he calls the zone of proximal development, an area of difficulty just above what the student can do alone. In this zone, a "more knowledgeable other" is needed to support the learning with the goal of making the child able to work at this same level without assistance. Any activities designed to be completed independently should, therefore, be at levels *below* this essential learning zone. These, then, are activities—not instruction. They are meant to reinforce what has already been learned.

When I travel the country and talk to other teachers, they are quick to admit that many of their students are not really reading during independent reading time. They also acknowledge that the students most likely to be "pretend reading" are the students who most need increased amounts of reading to catch up with their peers. Time dedicated to independent silent reading that is unmonitored and unsupported provides no guarantee that students actually read or grow as readers.

However, in the nearly twenty years that I have spent in classrooms where teachers use the bulk of instructional time to confer with students who are reading silently in self-selected texts, I have seen incredible growth in readers at all levels of competence and have seen reluctant readers transformed into avid ones. Intermediate and middle school students are still learning to read. Meeting with them individually to help them clarify their thinking continually results in great gains in both proficiency and engagement.

Handing Over Responsibility to Students

One July day several years ago, my principal called and asked me if I would meet a newly hired teacher at school to show her around our literacy center and answer some questions she had. The teacher was an excellent choice—professional, knowledgeable, and committed to the success of her students. But she had serious doubts about implementing a curriculum based on self-selected texts.

Nervously and in all sincerity, she looked at me and said, "How am I supposed to build background knowledge for seventy-five different books?"

Teachers—with all the best intentions—often take on responsibilities that actually belong to their student readers. Psychologists often call this *overfunctioning*, but no matter what it is called, it's an occupational hazard of this profession. In the real world of reading, no one appears when readers choose a book for which they have no background knowledge and provides a combination of lecture, pictures, and short texts to prepare for the reading of the book. Real readers choose books set in foreign settings or in situations very different from their own because they like to vicariously experience other lives or learn something about a topic with which they are totally unfamiliar.

No one sat young readers down before they read the first book in the Harry Potter series and gave them quick background knowledge on magic potions and sorcerers and an overview of the characters they would meet. They couldn't—because no adults had read the book first and planned units of study—a reality for which millions of children were probably grateful. *It was the discovery of these things on their own* that has woven the spell over so many children worldwide.

Dovetailing Independent Reading in the Balanced Literacy Classroom

Master craftsmen understand the meaning of the word *dovetail*. In carpentry, it is a perfectly designed juncture between two segments of a piece of furniture, the tabs in one interlocking perfectly with the notches in the other. When I hear this term, I picture a table so well crafted that it's easy to take for granted the support beneath the table's surface. Teachers, too, are craftsmen. I picture a teacher crafting a balanced literacy program that interlocks a series of instructional activities with such skill that students move from dependence to independence, always supported by their teacher's steady hand. Too often in classrooms I see students' reading stamina and engagement buckle like weak table legs during independent reading because they haven't been given enough support. Independent reading time has become instead a pleasant add-on instructional flourish that is not a part of the architecture of instruction.

The instruction in a balanced literacy classroom is built upon Gallagher and Pearson's theory (1983) of the gradual release of responsibility. The control of four elements in an instructional reading experience—the text, the decoding, the focus, and the application of skills and strategies—is initially assumed by the teacher and then gradually turned over to the students (Figure 1–1).

Instructional Format	Purpose	Level of Text	Level of Support

Read-Aloud	• Models fluent reading and builds listening comprehension
	• Demonstrates proficient reader skills and strategies
	• Introduces variety: new genres and more sophisticated texts
		Varies according to purpose	The teacher
			  • chooses the text
			  • chooses the focus
			  • decodes the text
			  • models application of the targeted skill or strategy
			Instruction is provided in a **whole-group** setting.

Shared Reading	• Models fluent reading
	• Builds students' sight vocabularies
	• Focuses student efforts on proficient reader skills and strategies
		Varies according to purpose	The teacher
			  • chooses the text
			  • chooses the focus
			  • decodes the text or shares the decoding with capable students
			  • assesses and coaches students as they apply the targeted skill or strategy
			Instruction is provided in a **whole-** or **small-group** setting.

Guided Reading	• Shifts responsibility to students to decode and apply skills and strategies *with the guidance of the teacher*
	• Introduces students to new genres and increased text sophistication *with the guidance of the teacher*
	• Addresses the specific group's comprehension and decoding needs
		Instructional
		93–98 percent known words
			The teacher
			  • chooses the text
			  • chooses the focus
			  • assesses and coaches students as they decode
			  • assesses and coaches students as they apply the targeted skill or strategy
			Instruction is provided in a **small-group** setting.

Supported Independent Reading	• Provides an opportunity for students to read individually in self-selected texts
	• Provides an opportunity for students to orchestrate and apply decoding and targeted skills and strategies *with teacher support as needed*
	• Addresses the individual comprehension **and engagement** needs of each individual student
		Instructional the majority of the time
		93–98 percent known words
		
		Independent occasion-ally to build fluency and confidence
		98–100 percent known words
			The teacher
			  • assesses students' engagement and comprehension
			  • coaches when students confront engagement or compre-hension challenges
			  • provides individualized instruction at students' point of need
			Instruction is provided in a **one-on-one** deskside conference.

Free Voluntary Reading	To give students an opportunity to read self-selected texts purely for pleasure	Varies according to students' choices	This may occur in any setting—inside or outside the school day.

Figure 1–1 *Layers of Support in a Reading Classroom*

When skills or strategies are introduced, the teacher controls all four elements: choosing a text that fits the lesson's focus, reading it aloud, and applying the skills or strategies during direct instruction while students watch and learn. In shared reading, the teacher continues to control the text and set the focus. The decoding workload is minimized by having the teacher or another capable reader read the text aloud. Students are encouraged to apply the skill or strategy being taught but the teacher steps in and takes control at points of confusion. In guided reading, the teacher relinquishes responsibility for decoding but continues to choose the text and the focus for reading. Application of the target skills or strategies during guided reading is assessed, and students are prompted as necessary to help them apply them on their own.

The traditional balanced literacy model moves from guided to independent reading once the teacher perceives that readers are ready to try a skill or strategy on their own, but there must be a level between these two instructional configurations in which the developing reader works with the *support* rather than the *guidance* of the teacher. When students are *guided*, the teacher is out in front of them, pulling them along a path the teacher has selected. However, when they are *supported*, the students are in the lead and someone is beside them to help accomplish a task they have chosen themselves. This level of instruction is supported independent reading.

Supported independent reading is similar to guided reading (Figure 1–2) but gives control of the text, the decoding, the focus, and the application over to the students. In both instructional configurations, the teacher is there to assist students as they try to decode and to apply skills and strategies independently. Deskside conferences during supported independent reading, however, meet the students' needs, not the teacher's. The students are in control—but, much like training wheels on the bike of a rider who is learning, the teacher is there to help steady the developing readers should they wobble and appear ready to fall. Supported independent reading, then, is reading done in mostly self-selected texts that are written at appropriate levels to spur growth in which the actual reading of the texts is monitored by a teacher who intervenes as necessary to ensure success.

It is essential that I monitor students during independent reading time. Left to their own devices, many of the readers in the room will choose other activities to fill their time, activities they have already learned to enjoy, such as sleeping, daydreaming, writing notes, or bothering their friends. There are not enough truly engaged readers in the typical classroom to make independent reading time productive without this essential supervision.

Guided Reading	Supported Independent Reading
The teacher works with a small group of four to six students.	The teacher works one-on-one with students.
The text is chosen by the teacher.	The text is chosen by the student with teacher guidance as needed.
The focus of the instruction is predetermined by the teacher and is the same for every member of the group.	The focus is determined by student responses and behaviors during a one-on-one conference and is individualized.
The teacher focuses attention on a small group for 15–30 minutes while other students work alone.	The teacher focuses attention on all students as needs arise.
Students are expected to do the decoding work and apply targeted skills and strategies with teacher support.	Students are expected to do the decoding work and apply targeted skills and strategies with teacher support.
The teacher controls the learning.	The student controls the learning.

Figure 1–2 *Comparison of Guided and Supported Independent Reading*

The Difference a Change Can Make

The eighth-grade assistant principal greeted me at the door one morning halfway through my first semester in the middle school I went to in 2006. "Can you explain to me why kids are coming into my office and wanting to talk about *books*? I've worked with these kids for over two years, and none of them has ever wanted to talk about books before. What is going on?"

The eighth graders who most frequently visited her office now wanted to talk to her about the books they were reading—and to encourage her to read them as well. They were taking books home with them and creating more space in their lives for reading. In December of that year, dozens of them ordered complete sets of Townsend Press' Bluford High series to read over the holiday *and* to give as gifts. One mother even called the school to see if the book order was real—she couldn't believe her daughter wanted money to buy *books*.

What transformed these students? The teachers in that middle school had taken a chance. They had quit relying on whole-group novels and books on tape and begun to implement supported independent reading. They took a leap of faith and trusted that this way of teaching would work.

And that change has made all the difference.

Questions for Reflection

As you consider the possibility of making this change in your classroom, here are some questions to consider:

- How many students are you *certain* have actually read the texts you so carefully selected?

- How accurately can you describe the challenges these texts have presented to individual students?

- How much do *your* activities drive students' interactions with texts and their pacing through them?

- How well can you describe the strengths and weaknesses of the individual readers in your classroom?

- How many of your students seek you out to talk about what they are reading?

- How often do you respond with the title of a book when someone asks what you are teaching?

If your answers to any of these questions cause you concern, you are ready to take the leap. Both you and your students will be glad you did.

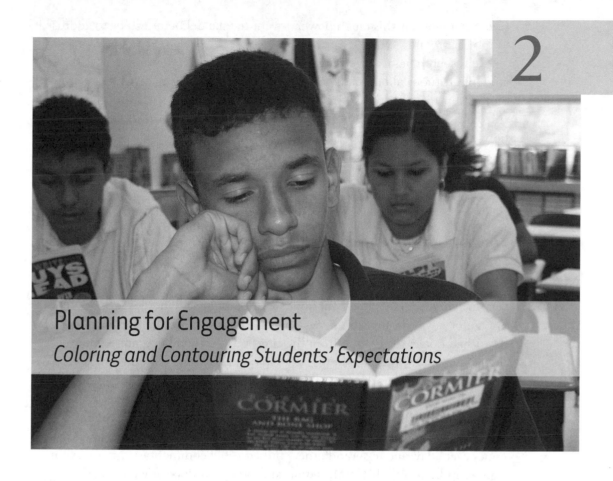

Planning for Engagement
Coloring and Contouring Students' Expectations

A cover article entitled "What's Hot, What's Not for 2007" in the March 2007 issue of *Reading Today* included motivation on its list of what was *not* currently "hot" in reading education (Cassidy and Cassidy 2007). I was astounded. How could these dedicated professionals downplay the role that engagement plays in building reading proficiency and a lifelong love of reading?

Any time there is a question in reading, I am convinced that engagement is the answer. According to Guthrie and Wigfield (2000), "As students become engaged readers, they provide themselves with self-generated learning opportunities that are equivalent to several years of education. Engagement in reading may substantially compensate for low family income and poor educational background" (404). Allington (2001) contends that "engagement in reading has been found to be the most powerful instructional activity for fostering reading growth" (37).

If engagement has this much power, I want to take deliberate steps to address it in my classroom.

No research has changed my teaching more than McKenna's work (2001) on student attitudes about reading. He identified three factors that impact student motivation to read: the student's prior reading experiences, the culture that surrounds the student both at home and at school, and the student's expectations about the reading experience. I have changed my teaching to address these factors because I now believe that expectations, which are affected by prior experiences and literacy cultures, are the key to engagement.

Students' Prior Experiences

I am grateful every day for the reading culture into which I was born. My mother was an avid reader and filled our home with Perry Mason mysteries and Frank G. Slaughter novels. She read the newspaper and several women's magazines every day. I had books read to me from the time I can remember—and we never left the grocery store without a new Little Golden Book to take home and enjoy. We made weekly trips to the library, purchased books from book fairs, and talked about the Nancy Drew books we had both read. And when I visited my grandparents, the walls of their house were literally lined with books, including the yellow-paged books my mother had read as a child. My grandmother read for hours every day, and my grandfather studied Bible commentaries every evening. I grew up believing that both fiction and nonfiction books were treasures and time spent reading was time well spent.

Once I entered school, learning to read was easy for me because my family had already created the conditions for my success. However, I have worked in Title I schools for the past twenty years. Very few of the students there have had the benefit of the wonderful reading examples I had growing up. They have childhoods and challenges very different from mine. The libraries are closed by the time their parents finish working multiple jobs—and there is no spare money for books with so many mouths to feed.

Students with limited exposure to books enter school with a significant disadvantage and lag behind in reading skills and language development (Neuman and Dickson 2006). They start out behind children who have had more experiences with texts. Unless they can build a clear vision of themselves as readers, these students may well lose their desire to do the hard work that catching up will entail.

Shaping Students' Concept of *Reader*

My husband is a very capable reader. He can make sense of engineering reports and proposals whose details overwhelm me. He can glean important information on current events from newspapers and magazines. But as good as he is at all of this, for him reading is merely a tool. He is not what I consider a reader.

If I want my students to be engaged with texts, I have an obligation to create a clear vision for them of what it means to be a *reader*. In guided reading groups and direct instruction, teachers have continually focused on what *good* readers do, but many students long ago gave up a vision of themselves as good readers. In fact, they don't consider themselves to be readers at all. If I can reshape the students' visions of themselves *as* readers, the change in their habits and attitudes will result in great gains in both engagement and proficiency.

Do All Readers Lug Heavy Tote Bags? Modeling the Behavior of a Reader

One of the first lessons I teach each school year is designed to clearly illustrate what I mean by the term *reader*. A piece of chart paper is posted at the front of the room as students enter. On it is written, "What is a reader?" Below this question is the stem sentence, "Readers . . ."

I begin class by letting students contribute ideas to this chart. Typically, students will tell me that readers can read all the words, that they understand what they read, that they use their strategies. In this age of No Child Left Behind, students now add that readers can read fluently when they read out loud. Usually, someone will add that readers read a lot—I'm always happy to add that one to the chart. As students offer ideas for me to write on the chart paper, I begin to get a picture of their previous experiences with and expectations for reading.

Once I have collected the student ideas, I tell them proudly that I am a *reader*—dramatically emphasizing the last word in the sentence. I tell them I am going to talk about what I do that makes me claim this title—and that afterward we'll see if there's anything we need to add to our chart.

At this point I drag—and I do mean *drag*—a huge canvas bag out from behind my desk. In the bag are magazines, the arts section of the Sunday paper, children's books, adult books, professional books, and graduate textbooks. In the bag are both books I love and those I hate. I sit down in a chair and begin to talk about all the things I am reading right now—everything from magazines and newspapers to professional books, young adult literature, nonfiction bestsellers, college texts, and "beach reads."

I always try to show both fiction and nonfiction and talk briefly about genre. I talk about how I read a lot of different things all at the same time—and tell them that my husband doesn't understand this at all. He thinks I should finish one book before I start another—but, then, he is not a reader!

I always make it a point to include books I didn't finish reading. My most common choices are *The Corrections* by Jonathan Franzen and *The Life of Elizabeth* by Alison Weir. I bought the Franzen book because of Oprah—and I really tried to read it. I read more than a hundred pages before I decided I just didn't like it enough to finish. I didn't care about any of the characters—I found all of them annoying—and Franzen's writing style just wasn't to my taste. I know several people who read and loved this book, but it just wasn't right for me. It is important for students to know that they don't *have* to like the same books as their friends.

I bought the Weir book because it is on one of my favorite topics—Queen Elizabeth I. But this text just had too many intricate details for me. I got bogged down in all the page-long descriptions of feasts and political documents. Again, I read nearly half the book before I decided it would be one I would not finish.

Students are always very surprised to learn that I don't finish every book I start. I believe sharing this part of my reading process is important. When they begin their independent reading, they, too, will want to abandon books. I make sure I give good, clear reasons why I chose the book and why I decided not to finish it. If they want to make the same choice, they need to provide the same types of information—why they chose the book, what they expected it to be, and why the book didn't live up to their expectations. Just telling me, "It's boring," is not going to fly. This also gives me the chance to stress the fact that I want them to *enjoy* what they read.

The last books I show them are the ones I've had to buy for graduate classes. These are books I didn't choose to read—someone else required them—and they are often books with which I had to struggle with very unfamiliar content. I spend some time talking about how much harder it is to read a book I don't choose for myself, especially if I will be expected to prove that I not only read it, but understood it. Students are, of course, surprised to find out that I sometimes struggle with my reading—but it is an important point to make. They need to understand that a *reader* will find ways to make text make sense no matter what.

After the lesson, the students and I add to the anchor chart we have started, specifically detailing the behaviors of readers (Figure 2–1). This chart stays up in

Readers . . .

- read many different kinds of texts.

- always have a purpose for their reading—and read for many different purposes.

- sometimes read more than one book at a time.

- finish books.

- like to own books.

- know what they will read next.

- get ideas about what to read next from magazines, newspapers, television, awards lists, book stores, and other readers.

- have favorite books and authors.

- reread books they love.

- don't finish books they don't like—but they give them a good try first and know exactly why they didn't like them.

- know what to expect from the type of book they're reading.

- read books they didn't choose differently from books they chose for themselves.

- slow down and reread when the text is hard.

- ask for help if the text just isn't making sense.

Figure 2–1   *Sample Anchor Chart on Behavior of Readers*

the classroom throughout the year—and I refer to it often when talking to students about both the good and bad decisions they are making as readers. My goal is not to create *good* readers—that will take care of itself if I can create *true* readers who read for joy.

Windows on Their World: Reading Autobiographies

The best tool I have found for understanding my students' prior experiences is the reading of autobiography (Figure 2–2). I wait until about the third week of school before asking students to complete this assignment. I will be asking them to share very personal stories and want their honesty, but they will not feel comfortable sharing until I have developed a climate of trust in my classroom. This can't happen in a day.

Questions for Reading Autobiographies

1. What memories do you have about reading and books from before you ever started school? It's okay if you don't have any, but mention that you don't.

2. Do you remember learning how to read? When? Was it hard or easy?

3. What have your experiences with reading in school been like? Tell the good and the bad—both are very important.

4. How have you felt about the read-aloud times in your classrooms? Are there any books you have enjoyed?

5. Do you have a favorite book or author? Talk about them.

6. What do you feel are your strengths as a reader? You have them, you know! Find at least one—but hopefully more.

7. What would you like to be able to do as a reader? Give me some good ideas on how to help you.

Figure 2–2 *Prompts Students Can Use to Reflect*

Students write their autobiographies in class. I want honesty—and sometimes parents steer their children away from statements they think put themselves in a bad light or reflect badly on previous teachers. I don't want censorship—I want the students' true perspectives on what their experiences have been.

The day before we write in class, I show students the questions they will be asked to answer and share my own answers to these questions (Figure 2–3). I do not polish my writing. I want the tone to be conversational and sincere, not professional quality. I answer honestly and make sure to go into depth in answer to the questions I have posed—and I write a new model every year so that my lesson will not seem canned and predictable. I continually emphasize that their autobiography will be draft writing. I am interested in the content of the piece, not the mechanics.

I try to be sure I include information on how my family's attitude about reading served to shape my own, how the assignments and texts my teachers chose affected my attitude toward reading, and how much I preferred books I had chosen myself to those my teachers assigned. While I show my own answers to the questions, I continually stress that their experiences may be very different from mine. This does not mean their reflections are better or worse—just different. I try to help them see how important it is for me to understand exactly what each of their reading experiences have been.

Mrs. Allison's History as a Reader

I guess my first memory of reading is when my mom used to read me bedtime stories. Every time we went to the grocery store she would buy me a Little Golden Book. These are the books she read to me at nap and bedtime. When I went to my grandparents' house, I got a special treat. They had all the books my mom read when she was a little girl. These were big, thick chapter books with not a lot of pictures, but they were still fun to look at.

I learned to read in first grade. My teacher was Mrs. Boehme, and I adored her. She was old and wrinkly—but she was good! I remember we were in reading groups and we read the Dick and Jane books. I still remember being the one whose turn it was to read when we saw our first two-syllable word. The word was *funny*, and I had no idea what it was. How embarrassing! But no one else knew the word, either, so I felt better.

I guess reading was always easy for me. I really wanted to learn to read all those books I had seen at home and at my grandmother's. And I instantly loved reading. My parents got me a library card, and I was always checking books out and in. Mom kept on buying me books at the grocery store, so that was fun. But when I got to high school I didn't usually enjoy the books I was required to read. I read them— but I always had another book going on the side that I enjoyed more. I hated *Silas Marner* so much in tenth grade that I refused to read it. I failed that test!

I always loved being read to. I guess that started with my mom. My sixth-grade teacher, Mrs. Jones, read to us for over an hour every Friday afternoon—we ALL loved it. She read us the Little House on the Prairie books and *Richard Halliburton's Book of Marvels*. And she read us poetry. My favorite was "Johnny's History Lesson." Everything happened in 1492!

My favorite book is *Wuthering Heights* by Emily Bronte. I have read it about fifty times. It has everything—ghosts, romance, revenge. It was written a long time ago, so it isn't an easy read—but I just love it!

I'm basically a good reader. I love reading and usually have several books going at the same time. I read in a lot of different genres and like to talk about what I read with my friends. I wish I was better at reading science articles. Sometimes I just get bogged down in them—but I'm working on it.

Figure 2–3   *A Sample Autobiography*

As I read these histories, I am looking for four specific elements that have played a role in shaping the students' current attitudes toward reading:

1. the reading challenges and successes they have encountered so far

2. the reactions their teachers and peers have had to them as readers

3. the expectations of their previous teachers

4. the ownership they have taken of their own literacy.

I do not grade these papers—I just read them. I offer no comments back at all. But as I work with students the rest of the year, I have their own experiences as reference points to help them mark their personal growth as readers.

Inviting Students into the Reader's World

On the first day of school when students enter the room, I want them to find themselves engulfed in a world of reading. Books are everywhere—lined up along the chalk trays, organized in shelves and baskets along the walls, placed in stacks or book boxes in the center of desks. The first thing I do with my classes each year is read to them.

My favorite read-aloud for the first day of school is *Book* by George Ella Lyon. This engaging picture book uses a series of metaphors to show what books offer dedicated readers. It sets the stage for a school year that will be spent reading books we love. Another picture book by Lyon, *A Sign*, can preface a discussion of why authors write books and how they attempt to connect to readers. Students often forget that at some point in time another human being actually sat down and put the words they are reading on paper, anticipating these words would someday be read and enjoyed. Other good books that build the foundation of a reading community are *Miss Malarky Leaves No Reader Behind* by Judy Finchler, *Wolf!* by Becky Bloom, and *Edward and the Pirates* by David McPhail. Although students may have encountered these books before, the ideas they present about reading's place in students' lives is well worth revisiting.

Book Talks: Plot Teaser Moments That Motivate

To become true readers, my students must be excited about books. I frequently dangle enticing books in front of readers in book talks and invite them to explore them on their own. These teasers usually involve a quick overview of the book's content followed by the reading aloud of a particularly engaging section or chapter from the book itself, a selection designed to leave the students clamoring for more. Lesesne considers book talks "personal introductions between books and readers" (2003, 114). Atwell, whose students rank book talks as a key factor in reading engagement, says that by regularly incorporating book talks in their classrooms, teachers "bring life, with our voices, to the tattered spines that line the shelves of our libraries" (2007, 67). I'd add that book talks are inherently warm, personal exchanges between teachers and students where the sociability of reading is front and center. Teacher authority relaxes a bit, and for a delayed reader, it is much like being warmly greeted at a party full of strangers and welcomed into their circle of conversation. Suddenly, you belong.

I present book talks at least once a week—more often if time allows. This requires me to be constantly on the lookout for books that will hook the readers in my room. I try to be aware of the genres, authors, and topics that are currently popular and look for titles my students have not discovered yet. I am always thinking ahead of the students, searching for new genres and authors that will motivate them to try increasingly more sophisticated texts. And I'm thinking of particular students, forever on the lookout for *that* book that will work for *that* child. I ask other teachers and our school librarian for recommendations—and the students overhear these conversations. These reading-centered conversations and frequent classroom book talks are substantial proof to my students that I am a reader, too.

It is amazing what a teacher recommendation can do. One sixth-grade teacher in my building recommends books through quick book talks almost every day—and says that the books she has highlighted are the first ones students choose. I always highlight a specific author before taking my students to the library. I give a brief biography, choose a specific title from her work, and then read an excerpt. Finally, I post a list of the author's books on the reading bulletin board. The school librarian finally asked me to start giving her several days' notice of what author I would be recommending so she could pull the books and have them on a cart instead of being bombarded by students with requests for those titles.

Students, too, can present book talks either in small-group book sharing or at the beginning of class. Their format should follow what the teacher has modeled—an overview that does not give away the ending, followed by a quick read-aloud to whet readers' appetites. Recommendations by peers often lead even reluctant readers to titles that they expect to enjoy. They are one more powerful tool that helps engage student readers.

Daily Exchanges: Sustaining Engagement, Confirming Membership

The teacher is only one person in the classroom; the actual community must include each individual student. It is not enough for teachers to be readers. They must help the students see themselves as readers as well. Lyons (2003) points out that one key to developing motivation to read is helping students form an attachment to others in the room. To accomplish this goal, the greatest tool at a teacher's disposal is classroom talk.

To set the stage for talk about books, I greet students at the door on the first day of school and ask, "Did you read any good books over the summer?" Then throughout the year, I continue to talk to students about texts. If I read something students might like, I recommend it or, if possible, put the actual book or article in students' hands. If there are books on student desks, I ask about them—particularly if I haven't read them yet. I usually say, "I haven't read this one. Is it any good?" I then pick up the book and read the back, demonstrating one more time how a reader previews books. If I *have* read the book, I ask what part the student is on and tease him with what is coming next. These casual conversations about books become a normal part of the school day and help build a reading bond between my students and me.

A reluctant student with whom I worked was reading *The Dollhouse Murders* by Betty Ren Wright. He had pulled the book from the classroom library, intrigued by both the title and my recommendation. Wright, however, takes a long time to set up the story and get to what the student was waiting for—the scary part. I merely asked, "Have the dolls started moving in the dollhouse yet? It's coming up soon, you know." That was all it took to keep him reading.

Centering teacher-to-student talk on books gives me an opportunity to connect to each of my students, even the more unruly ones. A short, informal conversation about books with the student who yesterday spent the entire day acting out can change the tone of our relationship and clearly communicate that today is a new day and his growth as a reader is more important than any classroom disruption he may have caused.

Conversations about books are nonthreatening and informal. These interplays are one-on-one, a personal moment in each day for each child. They can happen anywhere—at the classroom door, at student desks, in the hallway, at lunch. But they should happen regularly for every student—and with time they help develop a sense of trust between my students and me.

As I continue to hold conversations with students about books, a strange phenomenon occurs. Other students begin to join in. They eavesdrop and become interested in what we're saying. Suddenly they jump in with comments like, "I've read that book before—it's great!" or "Can I read that book when you're finished?" The stage has been set for a classroom community that focuses on reading.

When these informal discussions start, I introduce the "Books I Want to Read" sheet (Figure 2–4). These sheets are kept in student reading folders and checked regularly to see which students are actually listing titles there—and if they follow up by actually reading the book. When students plan what they will read next, they are becoming true readers.

Engaging Students Through Small-Group Sharing

I have found that the reading momentum in a classroom is accelerated when students regularly meet in informal small groups to talk about what they are currently reading. Unlike Book Clubs (Raphael, Pardo, and Highfield 2002) and Literature Circles (Daniels 2002), students in these groups have usually all read different books. The talk here centers around the common elements of the books—and introduces students to a wide variety of texts they otherwise might not have known.

I choose sharing groups based on the types of books students are reading. Students who are all reading fiction can discuss the character traits of their book's main character and how these traits affect the plot, or look at the central problem and how the main character is trying to solve it. Nonfiction readers can share the most interesting new things they've learned, how the graphics in the book convey important information, or how the text itself is structured. Students who are reading the same genre can share how their particular book exemplifies the characteristics of that genre. Sometimes, I mix students so everyone is reading a different kind of book. In this grouping, the readers talk about why they chose that book and what they like or don't like about it. I always eavesdrop on these student conversations, taking notes about things I want to discuss with individual readers later. I also join groups to discuss something I have read or offer insights into the discussions.

I recently listened in as a group of sixth graders discussed the fiction books they were reading. Their teacher had given a minilesson on the terms *protagonist* and *antagonist*, and this was to be the focus for their discussions. Steven wanted input from his group on the book he was reading, *A Living Nightmare: Book 1 in the Saga of Darren Shan*. "The main character in my book just can't be the protagonist!" he insisted. "I mean, this guy is just *not* a nice person. *Nobody* would call him a hero."

The students discussed this idea for a few minutes, listening as Steven detailed all the less-than-admirable qualities the character possessed. As confusion

Name: _____

Period: _____

BOOKS I WANT TO READ

Title	Genre	Author (F)/Call Number (NF)

Figure 2–4 *Books I Want to Read Sheet*

settled over the group, one boy wondered, "Do you think another character might actually be the protagonist—and you just missed it?"

"No, this guy is definitely the main character," Steven insisted. "So shouldn't he be the protagonist, too?"

About that time their teacher arrived to take advantage of a very important teachable moment. First she explained to the group that the protagonist is the person whose problem drives the action in the story—and that sometimes these characters are not very likeable people. Since readers know to expect the main character to change at some point in the story, it is possible he could become a better person, but that certainly is not always the case. She asked Steven to predict whether the character might change for the better, basing his answer on evidence from the book he was reading.

At the end of the small-group time, the teacher brought her discussion with Steven's group to the entire classroom, much like a soccer player thwacks the ball to a forward to expertly kick it right into the goal. The teacher knew she had a winning point that would heighten every student's understanding. Steven shared his dilemma and what he had learned from the teacher's comments. You could feel the impact in the class—this shift as students recognized that equating main character with goodness or heroism wasn't quite enough. When these students encounter Macbeth and Othello in their high school English classes, they will not be surprised that even classic protagonists sometimes exhibit far-from-sterling qualities. One spends a lifetime discovering and rediscovering that the writer's trick is to create a character that is sympathetic enough—even if he is not likeable. As readers we can then discuss whether there are times when we don't like a book because we don't sympathize with the character sufficiently. Is it okay to stop reading a book because of this? What are other reasons for not engaging with a novel?

The Difference Engagement Can Make

I met Juan the first day he returned from our district's alternative school. He was certainly not any teacher's dream. He walked with a swagger, often smirked at adults, and in general was in school more to enhance his social life than to increase his knowledge. By the end of the year, his behavior had landed him in the alternative program yet again.

He started his eighth-grade year at the alternative campus, but when he returned several weeks later his advisory teacher, a superb language arts teacher, introduced him to the Bluford High series from Townsend Press. She believed these would be the books that would finally win him over. Steering him toward engaging texts that spoke to his interests and needs was the first step in creating an eager reader.

One day I substituted in his advisory class so his teacher could attend a meeting. When I called roll I was amazed to see Juan's name on the class list. In my experience I had always known him to make a disruptive entrance. Assuming he was absent, I scanned the room. There he was—sitting in a chair in a corner, book in hand, reading. I stared in amazement—this surely couldn't be the same Juan! When the other students began to file out of class at the end of the period, Juan remained there in his chair—still reading. I walked over to him and quietly said, "Juan, advisory is over. It's time to go to sixth period."

"Just give me a minute, miss," he answered. "I need to finish this chapter."

Juan had learned to be a reader. Engagement can change even the least likely of students.

Questions for Reflection

Comprehension is usually the primary focus of instruction in a reading classroom. But if teachers first address the issue of students' engagement with texts, both the volume and quality of student reading will increase.

As you consider the issue of engagement, let these questions guide your thinking:

- Are you aware of experiences in their pasts that have shaped the way your students feel about reading?

- Do you read enough children's and young adult literature to know what books might interest specific students or groups of students?

- Do you share your own reading life with your students as a way of developing their understanding of what readers do?

- Do you talk to your students regularly about what they are reading and provide time for them to have similar conversations with their peers?

- Would a visitor to your room instantly notice that the culture of the classroom centers on reading?

Changes to your instruction based on the answers to these questions can greatly increase the number of students in your classroom who find themselves joyfully lost in a book every day. This engagement will move them one step closer to becoming avid, lifelong readers.

Clever Matchmaking Between Students and Books

Several years ago, at their teacher's request, I escorted a group of five totally disengaged readers to the library, hoping to help them find a book they might enjoy. We sat down at a round table in the library to talk about how readers choose books. Their body language spoke volumes—they slumped in their chairs, arms crossed across their chests, heads thrown back. Heavy sighs filled the air.

"Tell me what kinds of books you like," I began.
"I don't like books," one particularly surly young man volunteered.
"Not even the books your teacher reads aloud to you?" I asked.
"Nope—I told you. I don't like *any* books," he continued.
"But your teacher requires you to read thirty minutes every day, doesn't she?"
"Yep."

"So what do you do?"

"Turn the pages and pretend."

"Do you check books out of the library?"

"Yep—our teacher makes us."

"Then what?"

"I put them in my desk and leave them there until we come back to the library. Then I turn them in."

"What do you read during class?"

"I just pull something off the teacher's shelf. I told you—I don't really *read* it—I just pretend."

"Have you ever read a book all the way through?"

"Are you kidding me?"

Students who are not yet readers get absolutely no benefits from trips to the library. Their frustrated teachers often remind me of Kevin Costner in the movie *Field of Dreams.* His character carved a baseball diamond into his cornfield because a mystical voice promised, "If you build it, they will come." Teachers of disengaged readers often seem to believe, "If you bring them, they will read." If only that were true!

Since students in an independent reading classroom will usually spend thirty minutes a day reading, they must learn to choose books they intend to finish and enjoy. Teaching students to choose texts wisely is a skill, and just like other reading skills, it must be taught.

Building a Robust Classroom Library

On the first day of school, I place books in my students' hands the moment they enter. They see books displayed in every conceivable nook and cranny. Stacks of them sit at their desks waiting to be previewed. Since research continually shows that access to books has a positive impact on reading achievement (Allington 2001; Krashen 2004), I want my students surrounded by both narrative and informational texts at all levels to address their varying interests and needs.

Teachers are not famous for their unlimited bank accounts, but this shouldn't stop anyone from creating an independent reading classroom. Those who have not yet built up an extensive library collection can find cost-effective ways to build their libraries.

Many schools have literacy centers where books are available for use in the classroom, so this is an excellent place to start. I shop half-price and used bookstores, garage sales, and library book sales to stretch my dollars. I also preview book club fliers and become a walking advertisement for the books offered there. The more books my students order, the more free titles I get with bonus points. I have added hundreds of books to my collection with my sales pitches.

There are other ways to build the collection that cost me absolutely no money at all. Periodically, I encourage students to bring in books they have at home that they are finished reading. At midyear, they can trade the books they've read for another title from my classroom library, giving it a fresh, new look. I sometimes give rewards such as free homework passes, extra computer time, lunch with the teacher, or extra in-class reading time for bringing in books. Parents will often donate books to a classroom book drive as well.

Libraries are another good resource. Our local public library allows teachers to check out stacks of books for up to six weeks. School librarians will often put together a cart of books that can be taken to the classroom for student checkout. No matter how it is done, filling the classroom with as many books as possible should be an essential goal of every reading teacher.

I talk regularly with my school librarian about the books that are popular at the moment, especially since I would not normally choose to read some of the authors and genres the kids love. But I can force myself to read them if it means I can place them in the right students' hands.

Books listed as Children's Choices or Young Adult Choices by the International Reading Association each year, the Quick Picks for Reluctant Young Adult Readers from the American Library Association, and those that win state book awards are always good choices. I regularly check Bill's Best Books on the ALAN (Assembly on Literature for Adolescents) website and find these recommendations to be very useful as well (see Figure 3–1 for this and other websites). Newbery Award books, Orbis Pictus nonfiction book award winners, and Michael L. Printz award winners for adolescent literature are also good additions to the classroom library. It is important to remember, however, that these award winners are chosen by adults, not young readers themselves, and are sometimes considered less interesting than those selected by students.

Teachers will also need to keep the age and sophistication of their student readers in mind since many of the books written for adolescents contain strong language and more adult situations that may not be appropriate for younger readers.

When teachers ask for advice on stocking their classroom libraries, I always recommend starting with authors who have written a number of books that seem to appeal to the students. If students enjoy the first book by an author, they can use this knowledge to help them choose another book by the same author. Authors such as Sharon Draper, Jerry Spinelli, and Gordon Korman write books at varying

Books Selected by Students Themselves

Children's Choice Awards from the International Reading Association
www.reading.org/Resources/Booklists/ChildrensChoices.aspx

Young Adult Choice Awards from the International Reading Association
www.reading.org/Resources/Booklists/YoungAdultsChoices.aspx

Books Selected by Adults

Newbery Award lists (intermediate and middle school readers)
www.ala.org/ala/mgrps/divs/alsc/awardsgrants/bookmedia/newberymedal/
newberyhonors/newberymedal.cfm

Orbis Pictus Award lists (nonfiction)
www.ncte.org/awards/orbispictus

Michael L. Printz Award lists (young adult books)
www.ala.org/ala/mgrps/divs/yalsa/booklistsawards/printzaward/Printz.cfm

ALAN's Picks from the Assembly on Literature for Adolescents
www.alan-ya.org

Quick Picks for Reluctant Young Adult Readers from the American Library
Association
www.ala.org/yalsa/booklists/quickpicks

Figure 3–1 *Websites to Guide Book Selections*

levels and even in various genres, so they are important to include in the classroom library. Finding an author they love is an important first step toward building students' lifetime love of reading. (See Figures 3–2 through 3–5 for more recommendations.)

Making the Classroom Library Accessible

Teachers arrange their classroom libraries in a host of different ways. Some just place books on shelves in no particular order; some put them in baskets or sections by genre. I personally like to arrange books by genre so that students can look for the type of book they already know they like.

Although Calkins (2001) makes a convincing argument for leveled libraries, I am still committed to the idea of teaching students to make correct choices

Recommended Fiction Series for Below-Level Intermediate Students

Junie B. Jones series by Barbara Park

Abby Hayes series by Ann Mazer

Geronimo Stilton series by Geronimo Stilton

Magic Treehouse series by Mary Pope Osborne

Recommended Nonfiction Series for Below-Level Intermediate Students

Magic Treehouse Research Guides by Will Osborne and Mary Pope Osborne

Matt Christopher Sports Biographies

High Five Reading series from Capstone Press

Disasters in History graphic series from Capstone Press

Recommended Fiction Series for Below-Level Middle School Students

The Bluford series from Townsend Press

Orca Currents series from Orca Book Publishers

Orca Sports series from Orca Book Publishers

Recommended Nonfiction Series for Below-Level Middle School Students

High-Performance series from Capstone Press

High Five Reading series from Capstone Press

Graphic Library from Capstone Press

Can Science Solve? series from Heinemann Library

Recommended Fiction Series for Middle School English-Language Learners

Carter High series from Saddleback Educational Publishers

Walker High Mysteries from Saddleback Educational Publishers

Figure 3–2 *Recommended Series for Below-Level Readers*

Avi	Dan Gutman	Katherine Paterson
Lynne Reid Banks	Margaret Peterson Haddix	Gary Paulsen
Judy Blume	Mary Downing Hahn	Richard Peck
Clyde Robert Bulla	Virginia Hamilton	Rodman Philbrick
Eve Bunting	Karen Hesse	Dav Pilkey
Betsy Byars	Dan Hiaasen	Willo Davis Roberts
Meg Cabot	Will Hobbs	Thomas Rockwell
Matt Christopher	James Howe	J. K. Rowling
Beverly Cleary	Joanna Hurwitz	Pam Munoz Ryan
Andrew Clements	Brian Jacques	Cynthia Rylant
Eoin Colfer	Peg Kehret	Louis Sachar
Ellen Conford	E. L. Konigsberg	Neal Shusterman
Caroline B. Cooney	Gordon Korman	William Sleator
Bruce Coville	Gail Carson Levine	Lemony Snicket
Sharon Creech	C. S. Lewis	Zilpha Keatley Snyder
Christopher Paul Curtis	Lois Lowry	Donald Sobol
Roald Dahl	D. J. MacHale	Gary Soto
Paula Danziger	Patricia MacLachlan	Jerry Spinelli
Barthe DeClements	Stephen Manes	R. L. Stine
Carl Deuker	Ann M. Martin	Mildred D. Taylor
Kate DiCamillo	Megan McDonald	Theodore Taylor
Lois Duncan	Phyllis Reynolds Naylor	J. R. R. Tolkien
Nancy Farmer	Jenny Nimmo	Wendelin Van Draanen
John D. Fitzgerald	Garth Nix	Bill Wallace
Sid Fleischman	Joan Lowery Nixon	Gertrude Chandler Warner
Cornelia Funke	Scott O'Dell	E. B. White
Jack Gantos	Mary Pope Osborne	Elizabeth Winthrop
Jean Craighead George	Christopher Paolini	Betty Ren Wright
Patricia Reilly Giff	Barbara Park	Laurence Yep
Jamie Gilson		

Figure 3–3 *Never-Fail Fiction Authors for Intermediate Classroom Libraries*

Laurie Halse Anderson	Linda Glovach	Joan Lowery Nixon
M. T. Anderson	Nikki Grimes	Scott O'Dell
Avi	Dan Gutman	Christopher Paolini
T. A. Barron	Margaret Peterson	Barbara Park
Joan Bauer	Haddix	Katherine Paterson
Judy Blume	Mary Downing Hahn	Gary Paulsen
Eve Bunting	Virginia Hamilton	Richard Peck
Betsy Byars	Karen Hesse	Rodman Philbrick
Meg Cabot	Dan Hiaasen	Celia Rees
Matt Christopher	Will Hobbs	Ann Rinaldi
Beverly Cleary	Anthony Horowitz	J. K. Rowling
Andrew Clements	James Howe	Willo Davis Roberts
Eoin Colfer	Joanna Hurwitz	Pam Muñoz Ryan
Caroline B. Cooney	Brian Jacques	Cynthia Rylant
Robert Cormier	Peg Kehret	Louis Sachar
Bruce Coville	David Klass	Neal Shusterman
Sharon Creech	E. L. Konigsberg	William Sleator
Chris Crutcher	Gordon Korman	Roland Smith
Christopher Paul Curtis	Kathryn Lasky	Lemony Snicket
Roald Dahl	Gail Carson Levine	Zilpha Keatley Snyder
Paula Danziger	C. S. Lewis	Donald Sobol
Barthe DeClements	Robert Lipsyte	Gary Soto
Sarah Dessen	Lois Lowry	Jerry Spinelli
Carl Deuker	David Lubar	R. L. Stine
Kate DiCamillo	D. J. MacHale	Todd Strasser
Sharon M. Draper	Patricia MacLachlan	Mildred D. Taylor
Lois Duncan	Stephen Manes	Theodore Taylor
Nancy Farmer	Ann M. Martin	J. R. R. Tolkien
Jean Ferris	Norma Fox Mazer	Wendelin Van Draanen
Sharon Flake	Megan McDonald	Cynthia Voigt
Sid Fleischman	Carolyn Meyer	Bill Wallace
Alex Flinn	Ben Mikaelson	E. B. White
Cornelia Funke	Walter Dean Myers	Elizabeth Winthrop
Jack Gantos	Phyllis Reynolds Naylor	Jacqueline Woodson
Gail Giles	Jenny Nimmo	Laurence Yep
Jamie Gilson	Garth Nix	Paul Zindel

Figure 3–4 *Never-Fail Fiction Authors for Middle School Classroom Libraries*

Robert D. Ballard	Joy Masoff
Matt Christopher	Jim Murphy
Jon Finkel	Walter Dean Myers
Russell Freeman	John Nichols
Robert Genat	Elizabeth Partridge
Gail Gibbons	Gary Paulsen
Michael Green	Andrea Davis Pinkney
Wilborn Hampton	Laurence Pringle
Chris Hayhurst	David West Reynolds
Cathy Hopkins	Tucker Shaw
Mark Huebner	Terry Sievert
Kathleen Krull	Seymour Simon
Gregory Leland	Diane Stanley
Julius Lester	Shelley Tanaka
Joel Levy	Jane Yolen
David MacCauley	

Figure 3–5   *Never-Fail Nonfiction Authors for Intermediate and Middle School Class-room Libraries*

without leveling, particularly in the intermediate and middle school grades. Book-stores and libraries don't put dots on book spines and direct readers to the correct colored dot. This commitment to student choice requires vigilance on my part. I have to know both the readers and the texts and must be willing to intervene when poor choices are made. But this more closely replicates reading in the world outside of school.

I believe that classroom library books are there to be read. And sometimes—no matter how vigilant the teacher might be—books disappear. I quit using a check-out system for my books years ago. If a book disappears from my shelf be-cause it went home with a student who wanted to read it, that—to me—is not only an occupational hazard but a tribute to the fact that I am giving students ac-cess to the books they truly want to read.

Do I lose some books every year? Of course I do. Even libraries with detector systems lose books. I am continually putting new titles on the shelves, so the few that are missing are regularly replaced. I write my name in black marker on the edge of the leaves on the right-hand side, so if the books are found in the hall-way or in lockers it is easy to return them to me.

The students know these books in my classroom are there for them. I think of them as the *students'* books and teach them to feel the same way. If they don't return a book they've borrowed, they have hurt the other students more than me. My commitment is to create an environment that nurtures readers, so I consider losing books a tribute to the time I have spent helping students learn to love reading. I don't expect every teacher to adopt this way of thinking—but it has made my classroom library a stress-free environment for me as well as for my students.

Planning for Student Choice

Choice is critical to student success and essential for motivation. In fact, Daniels and Bizar (2005) stress that students must learn "to make meaningful decisions and choices, living with all the consequences that choice entails" (26). But students cannot be expected to make informed choices if they are not aware of all the choices at hand. If their choices are ever going to matter, their expectations must change. Students who have grown accustomed to grabbing a random book from the shelf and later pretending to read it must be taught instead to expect to find a book there that they will love.

Early in the school year, I try to dazzle students with the endless variety of books available to them. I plan lessons that allow them to hold, preview, and skim through books from the classroom and school libraries, books that they can actually access when independent reading begins. I try to clarify and change their expectations for reading.

Skilled readers know what to expect when they open a mystery or a science fiction novel; they know nonfiction texts look very different from those in the fiction section. They also know these books are read differently as well. As Sibberson and Szymusiak (2003) point out, this is one reason why many struggling readers are confused from the moment they begin reading. Without a clear understanding of how texts are structured and what elements define a genre, they have no idea how to approach their reading.

Students need a cursory tour of a variety of texts so they know what genres might interest them. I help by offering opportunities for them to explore the popular genres of realistic fiction, mystery, horror, fantasy, science fiction, historical fiction, biography, and informational text one at a time in a series of lessons. These lessons teach them what to expect from each genre and give them time to explore books that I hope will grab their interest.

Creating Excitement About Fiction

I usually begin with realistic fiction since this is often the most accessible genre for students. I place an assortment of realistic fiction books at several stations in the classroom. The titles at each station represent a wide range of reading levels so that even the most challenged readers can find books at their level. Accelerated Reader lists, the backs of books, websites, and the school librarian are excellent sources to use to establish the levels and to be sure currently popular titles are included.

Each day, I give a brief book talk on three titles from the same genre that are written at various reading levels. On the first day, I have to be sure the students know that the term *genre* just means "a certain kind of book." Students need to understand that all books in a genre have common characteristics—and that by knowing what these characteristics are, readers know what to expect when they read the book. This is important prior knowledge that students must gain before reading.

I hold up each of the three books individually, starting with the easiest to read and ending with the most difficult. I read parts of each book aloud so the students can get a sense of the author's style and the type of vocabulary and sentence structure used.

I remind them that their reading level is an indication not of their intelligence but of how much time they have spent reading. They may be really interested in books that are too hard for them at the moment, so I coach them to consider those their target books—the ones they're working toward being able to read. I stress the importance of reading books that are just challenging enough to be manageable, books that will help them develop the skills and understandings they need to eventually read any book they choose. I assure them that reading books that are too difficult does not make them a better reader—it just makes them like reading less.

Together, the students and I build a chart of the characteristics of the genre of the day, including names of authors who write in that genre. (See Figures 3–6 and 3–7 for samples.) Historical fiction and science fiction will usually take more time because these genres are often more confusing for students. Characteristics should be focused on what to expect from the characters, the setting, and the events. When choosing books to highlight each day, I try to choose authors who have written several titles. Jerry Spinelli, Andrew Clements, and Sharon Draper have changed many reluctant readers' attitudes. Recurring characters such as Junie B. Jones and familiar settings such as the school-centered stories of Andrew Clement provide a degree of comfort for students as they grow as readers.

Genre	What to Expect	Authors in This Genre
Realistic fiction	• Setting is a familiar place (school, neighborhood, etc.) in current time. • Characters have problems similar to our own. • Events seem like they could actually happen to us or someone we know.	Paula Danziger Jerry Spinelli Lois Lowry Jack Gantos Andrew Clement Walter Dean Myers Sharon Draper
Adventure/survival	• Characters will be caught in a life-threatening situation and will need to use their wits to survive. • The setting is usually outdoors. • Events are the focus.	Gary Paulsen Will Hobbs Gordon Korman Jean Craighead George
Mystery	• There will be some type of crime or unexplained occurrence. • The main character will try to solve the mystery. • The author will leave clues to help the reader find the solution.	Joan Lowery Nixon Lois Duncan Caroline B. Cooney Jay Bennett Willo Davis Roberts
Horror	• Characters will have encounters with supernatural forces such as ghosts. • Events and setting will create a sense of fear in the reader.	Mary Downing Hahn R. L. Stine Betty Ren Wright Pam Conrad Darren Shan
Fantasy	• Characters often have magical powers (talking animals, wizards). • Events are purely imaginative and could never really occur. • The setting is often an imagined world.	Lynne Reid Banks Elizabeth Winthrop Eoin Colfer J. K. Rowling Christopher Paolini

Figure 3–6 *Sample Genre Charts*

(Continued)

Genre	What to Expect	Authors in This Genre
Science fiction	• The setting is often in the future or in a present that is very different from what we know. • Characters interact with creatures and technology that do not currently exist.	William Sleator Neal Shusterman Lois Lowry
Historical fiction	• The setting is in the past. • Real people and events may be mentioned—but the main characters aren't real. • Words that are no longer common may be used.	Lois Lowry Pam Muñoz Ryan Richard Peck Christopher Paul Curtis
Biography	• The events and people are real. • Only important events will be included.	Elizabeth Partridge Matt Christopher Milton Meltzer
Informational texts	• The whole book will be about one main topic and will not tell a story. • There will be specialized vocabulary words.	Russell Freedman Jim Murphy

Figure 3–6   (*Continued*)

Launch a Shopping Spree for a Perfect Match

Once the day's book talks are finished, it is time for a book shopping excursion. I tell the students they are about to become shoppers. The experience will be very similar to shopping for clothes or shoes because they will examine merchandise, looking for something that is a good "fit" for them. Clothes and shoes that don't fit properly are not comfortable to wear, just as books that don't fit properly aren't comfortable to read. I ask students to offer ideas about how they decide what shoes or clothes to try on. Usually, they mention wanting something that was seen in an advertisement, something that is a favorite color or pattern, or something that "everyone" is wearing. They also talk about how their choices fit their personal tastes and enjoyment.

Adventure/Survival		Science Fiction	
Jean Craighead George	Gordon Korman	K. A. Applegate	Neal Shusterman
Will Hobbs	Theodore Taylor	Margaret Peterson Haddix	William Sleator
		Lois Lowry	

Realistic Fiction		Fantasy	
Laurie Halse Anderson	Gordon Korman	Lynne Reid Banks	Mary Pope Osborne
Matt Christopher	Lois Lowry	T. A. Barron	Christopher Paolini
Andrew Clements	Ann M. Martin	John Bellairs	J. K. Rowling
Sharon Creech	Ben Mikaelson	Bill Brittain	Jon Sczieska
Paula Danziger	Walter Dean Myers	Eoin Colfer	Lemony Snicket
Sharon Draper	Barbara Park	Susan Cooper	J. R. R. Tolkien
Patricia Reilly Giff	Rodman Philbrick	Bruce Coville	Elizabeth Winthrop
Dan Greenburg	Louis Sachar	Brian Jacques	Jane Yolen
Carl Hiassen	Gary Soto	C. S. Lewis	Paul Zindel
S. E. Hinton	Jerry Spinelli		
Joanna Hurwitz	Cynthia Voigt		
E. L. Konigsburg	Bill Wallace		

Historical Fiction		Mystery/Suspense	
Avi	Lois Lowry	Avi	Richard Peck
Christopher Paul Curtis	Joan Lowery Nixon	Caroline B. Cooney	Christopher Pike
Karen Cushman	Richard Peck	Franklin W. Dixon	Marjorie Weinman Sharmat
Sid Fleischman	Pam Muñoz Ryan	Lois Duncan	Donald J. Sobol
Karen Hesse	Mildred Taylor	Mary Downing Hahn	R. L. Stine
		Anthony Horowitz	Gertrude Chandler Warner
		Phyllis Reynolds Naylor	Betty Ren Wright
		Joan Lowery Nixon	

Figure 3–7   *Sample Author/Genre Charts*

Then, I ask what a shopper should look at when choosing a book—its color? This provides a teachable moment that will ensure students know to preview a book by reading the teaser the publisher has provided and looking inside the book to gauge the level of vocabulary. Through this discussion, we come to the conclusion that a "good fit" book piques the reader's interest and is written at a level that presents enough challenges to grow but not so many challenges that it over-whelms the reader.

When I ask students how I can figure out what a book is about, they invariably tell me to look at the back of the book. I like to use my personal copy of *Burning Up* by Caroline Cooney at this point in the lesson because the back of it is totally blank. I want students to know that publishers sometimes put teasers on the inside flap of the book, so that they won't be confused if they encounter this in their own searches for their "just-right" books.

It is important to stress that after reading what the book is about, a book shopper must then decide if that book is worth trying on. If the book doesn't sound interesting, it is time to put it back on the shelf. But if it *does* sound like something that would be interesting to read, it's time to check and be sure it is at the right level.

I have seen many teachers assign students to a given reading level based on assessments done before going to the library. Students then become more interested in finding a book at the right level than in finding one they will actually enjoy reading. Finding a book that sounds good should be a reader's first step, not finding one at a predetermined level.

The best strategy I have found for helping students learn to find books at an appropriate reading level for them is the five-finger rule. It is really quite simple. Readers open books under consideration to a page somewhere in the middle of the book and skim down the page looking for words they don't know. Every time they find an unfamiliar word, they hold up one finger. If they have five fingers up at the bottom of the page, the book is too difficult. If they have no fingers up at all, the book is probably too easy and will not spur the desired growth.

Students should do this with two or three pages before deciding whether the book is at the right level for them to read. One page may not give a true picture of the book's level. Students also need to understand the meaning of the word *skim*. This strategy is a quick assessment—it shouldn't take a lot of time. If students are trying to actually *read* a text that is going to prove to be too hard, it will slow them down.

◎ The Fiction Shopping Spree

Once the students know how to preview a book and assess its reading level, they are ready to start "trying on" books. I give each student a Book Shopping Record Sheet (Figure 3–8). On this sheet, the students will write down the title and author of each book they preview, rating each on how interested they are in its content and how appropriate the reading level might be.

Name: _____

Period: _____

BOOK SHOPPING RECORD SHEET

Title	Author/ Call Number	Genre	Interest Level 3 = Very interested 2 = Kind of interested 1 = Not interested	Reading Level E = Too easy H = Too hard * = Just right

Some possible genres: Realistic fiction, science fiction, fantasy, mystery/suspense, adventure, historical fiction, biography, informational text

Figure 3–8 *Book Shopping Record Sheet*

© 2009 by Nancy Allison from *Middle School Readers*. Portsmouth, NH: Heinemann.

I discuss the fact that this is an *individual* decision—what is right for someone else may not be right for me. Both my daughter and I are readers—but she prefers science fiction, a genre I seldom choose to read. The books she loves are not good choices for me—but they are still good books.

Using a book from the classroom library as a model, I show students how to respond to the columns on the record sheet. Then the stacks of books are placed at various stations around the room and students begin previewing them. I walk through the room, talking to students about the various books and answering their questions. After about ten minutes, I give students a new stack of books so that the interest level stays high. This shopping expedition not only provides guided practice in finding just-right books but also creates a buzz of excitement about reading.

Book Talking Nonfiction

Teachers often underestimate the power of nonfiction to engage student readers. For example, I recently talked with a group of teachers who were trying to revamp their grade-level curriculum, which was almost completely dominated by fiction. At one point, I suggested they include a unit on nonfiction for the next year. One teacher groaned and said, "The kids just don't like nonfiction." That has not been my experience nor the experience of many researchers who have studied reluctant readers and middle school students (Jobe and Dayton-Sakari 1999; Carter and Abrahamson 1998; Lesesne 2006). I suspect this teacher's comment reflected her own tastes rather than her students'.

I spent at least two years when I was in the intermediate grades reading nothing but biographies. There was an entire area in our small school library filled with juvenile biographies, all with turquoise blue covers and the name of a famous person printed in red. I read about Clara Barton and Dolly Madison and Florence Nightingale, just to name a few. The real lives of these amazing women were much more interesting to me than any novel in the fiction section.

When I had time for choice reading in college, I read only nonfiction—anything I could find about the Kennedy assassination, true crime books, biographies of famous movie stars. Now, I spend much more time reading professional books and adult nonfiction than I do reading novels, even though I make time for both.

Many students, particularly boys and English-language learners, find nonfiction more compelling than fiction. Current series on high-performance vehicles and military weapons can often catch the attention of even the most reluctant boy, and language learners approach nonfiction with more background knowledge than they do fiction set in either contemporary or historic America. I must give my students the freedom to choose something they truly want to read—and many will choose nonfiction. If an entire week is spent previewing nonfiction, it is time well spent.

Biographies form the bridge between fiction and nonfiction. Both have a narrative structure that centers on people—fictional characters or living human beings. Both present information arranged in some type of time order.

Biographies, however, have a very different purpose from fiction, which must be discussed with students. Authors write fiction to engage readers in a story; they write biographies to share important details about real people's lives. The events in biographies are not likely to be as elaborately developed as those in fiction since the author's purpose is to inform rather than to entertain. Authors of biographies are limited to the factual details of their subject's lives, which aren't always easily available.

An introduction to nonfiction provides an excellent opportunity for me to point out the charts, graphs, and timelines that are included in many of the current biographies written for young people. It is also a chance for me to show students how to preview a nonfiction book.

When they previewed fiction books, students looked at the jacket notes, the backs of books, and chapter titles. For nonfiction books, they will also need to flip through the chapters and notice the headings, pictures, and graphics. They will need to look carefully at the table of contents and may even want to examine the index in the back.

I point out that nonfiction texts contain what is called *specialized vocabulary*, words that are only used when discussing whatever the topic might be. Often, there is a glossary in the back to help, or the words may be defined within the text. I need to make sure my students know that.

The Nonfiction Shopping Spree

As with fiction, I collect stacks of books for the students to preview, this time arranged by Dewey classification. I can't accurately describe the excitement that fills the room when students are exploring nonfiction. They discover titles such as *Oh, Yuck! The Encyclopedia of Everything Nasty* and *Oh, Yikes! History's Grossest Moments* by Joy Masoff, *The World's Fastest Trucks: Built for Speed* by Glen and Karen Bledsoe, Monica Hughes' Creepy Creatures series, Can Science Solve books from Heinemann Library, or the ever-popular books of world records. Books with cross-section illustrations such as *The AH-64 Apache Helicopter: Cross-Sections* by Ole Steen Hansen are always popular as well. During these book explorations, the only redirection I normally need to give is to ask students to give up a book because someone else wants to see it. Students want to begin reading the books right away.

Rather than being handed a sheet that explains the Dewey Decimal System, students enjoy the challenge of discovering the focus of the various numbered sections of the library on their own. The books at each station are all from the same numbered section of the library. Besides completing their book shopping sheets (Figure 3–8), I ask students to discover why these books would all be found in the same place in the library. Class discussions after these examinations result in an anchor chart that becomes a guide to the Dewey Decimal System to which the class can refer all year.

Book Shopping Record Sheets: Early in the Year Assessment Tools

While students are participating in a book shopping spree, I work the room. I notice who immediately dives into the books and who leans back away from the stack and then reluctantly picks a book to preview, acting as if it has been contaminated. I notice what books excite students the most. I listen to who says, "Oh, I've read this one!" multiple times and who never says it at all. This is the start of my assessment.

After the sprees have ended and the day is done, the assessment continues. I have the students' Book Shopping Record Sheets to review. These artifacts will tell me more about my students than any high-stakes test can ever show.

Each column on the book shopping sheet presents its own challenges for uncommitted readers, even columns asking for the book's title and the last name of its author. Many of today's books by popular authors feature the authors' names in letters bigger than the title of the book, which confuses many students not familiar with these writers. In a recent eighth-grade experience, many students were confused by Avi's *The Book Without Words*, which has the subtitle *A Fable of Medieval Magic by Avi*. Many, including some in the preadvanced placement class, were totally confused by the cover of this book, unsure what the book's title really was and who wrote it. Series books present yet another challenge as readers unfamiliar with a series assume the series title is the title of the individual book.

Confusions like these tell me what these students need to know. The students are unfamiliar both with popular writers of children's and young adult fiction and with the ways that subtitles can further shape their expectations for a text. They are unaware that books in a series will include both the title of the series, and the title and number of the individual book.

Based on this assessment, I know that my instruction will need to:

- show individual students how to use the title page to help them determine author and title

- present a short minilesson on series books and how their predictability can support readers who are looking for a book or an author to love

- expressly teach through a minilesson what a subtitle is and how it offers specific guidance from the author about what a reader can expect from a book.

◎ *Assessing Students' Genre Knowledge*

The genre column of the book shopping sheet gives me further insight into students' understanding of how knowledge of a genre shapes their expectations for reading. I recently worked in a sixth-grade class where the teacher had spent most of the previous week having students talk about genres and sort her classroom library into genre baskets. At the start of my lesson, I discussed the term and developed a list of characteristics of the four genres we were previewing that day.

Despite all of that, these students struggled with the book shopping spree. Even when I told them what types of books were in the baskets I was giving them, they still asked me what I meant by genre and what genre they had. This is clear evidence that these students did not understand how genre could shape their book choice and support their comprehension. They hadn't learned what we had taught because we hadn't taken the time to make this knowledge meaningful to them. Their confusions let me know that I needed to:

- help students develop clear understandings of and expectations for a number of different genres by reading aloud and discussing excerpts from a wide array of trade books

- explain how I use the publisher-supplied summary of the book to determine its genre

- demonstrate how I use my understanding of genre to shape my expectations for and comprehension of texts.

The genre column also helps me identify the strong readers in the room. On one of my recent book shopping sprees, an eighth-grade boy sat with a basket of realistic fiction books in front of him, dutifully recording titles on his record sheet and previewing each book. I happened to visit his table as he was previewing Gordon Korman's *No More Dead Dogs*. "Isn't this a humor book?" he asked.

Surprised by the depth of his genre knowledge, I smiled and said, "It sure is."

"Then why is it in a basket with realistic fiction?" he asked.

"Because life can sometimes be funny," I explained. "Realistic fiction can actually be broken down into even smaller categories such as sports fiction and animal stories, but all of it is fiction that seems real because the situations and characters are like those you know about in your own life and that of your friends." This student clearly understands the concept of genre in all its subtleties and is likely to be an engaged reader who knows how to pick books he intends to finish and enjoy.

◎ *Assessing Students' Interests*

The last two columns of the Book Shopping Record Sheet are the most valuable to me. They are intentionally arranged so that students determine their interest in a book before deciding if its reading level is appropriate for them, the same order in which they should approach these tasks in the library itself. When I explain this column on the Book Shopping Record Sheet, I always ask students how I can tell if I am interested in a book. Their answer is very often, "By looking at the cover."

I always hope for this response because it gives me an opportunity to discuss the importance of *not* judging a book by its cover. Some incredibly engaging older books are often ignored because their cover art is different from the more tabloid-inspired art currently adorning book covers. Publishers design covers to sell books, but covers can be deceiving. Students need to know it is important to read the summary on the back cover or dust jacket before deciding if they are interested in a book. Cover art alone is not enough information to make good choices.

The interest column is the one that gives me the most insight into the engagement level of students. I always spend time telling students their most important job when filling out a Book Shopping Record Sheet is to be honest. This sheet is a guide to books and authors they will love and a reflection of their reading habits and interests. I don't expect them to like all—or even any—of the books they preview; I just expect them to be honest about it.

When I put together collections for book shopping sprees, I try to always include books I consider instantly engaging. For intermediate students, I always plant Kate DiCamillo's *Because of Winn-Dixie*, Louis Sachar's *Holes* and *There's a Boy in the Girl's Bathroom*, Betty Ren Wright's *The Dollhouse Murders*,

Mary Downing Hahn's *Wait Till Helen Comes,* David Lubar's *Invasion of the Road Weenies: And Other Warped and Creepy Tales*, one Judy Moody book, one of Gordon Korman's survival series books, and a Goosebumps book or two. Middle school students will always find William Sleator's *Rewind*, Margaret Peterson Haddix's *Among the Hidden*, Joan Lowery Nixon's *Whispers from the Dead*, Caroline B. Cooney's *The Face on the Milk Carton*, Sharon Draper's *Tears of a Tiger*, David Lubar's *Sleeping Freshmen Never Lie*, a book from Darrin Shan's Cirque du Freak series, one from Gordon Korman's On the Run series, one from Meg Cabot's Princess Diaries series, and Anthony Horowitz's *Point Blank* among the books they will preview that day. These are books I have seen change students' attitudes about reading countless times—and I continue each year to look for more books that will be my trustworthy partners in leading students to a love of reading. If students don't find any of these books interesting, I know that they will need a great deal of attention early in the year.

Because I don't really know them yet, it can be hard for me to gauge the accuracy of a student who ranks every book she or he previews as "high interest." Some of them could be teacher pleasers who want to make a good impression and are giving me no insight into what genres interest them. But students who rank every book as "low interest" are showing who they truly are as readers. They either don't care enough to actually read the book summary because they are already convinced they don't like *any* books—or they read them with this conviction firmly set in their minds. These are the students who will see me first when deskside conferences begin—and they will confer with me every day until I feel they are engaged in a book that may change them as readers.

Assessing student responses to the interest column on the Book Shopping Record Sheet helps me know:

- which students will need considerable help learning to find books they will enjoy

- which genres interest which students

- which students are locked within a genre and will need help broadening their reading interests

- which students can serve as role models for other less engaged readers in the room

- which students can be grouped together for book discussions

- which books I need to have available in my classroom library.

◎ *Assessing Reading Levels*

The final column on the Book Shopping Record Sheet asks students to record whether or not the book they previewed was at the right reading level for them. This column gives me valuable insight into where my students are in their growth as readers. Students who continually rate what I consider to be on-level books as too hard are students who have not read enough or have not been given enough support and need to catch up with their peers. Sometimes these students are second-language learners who will catch up quickly as they consume more and more English words; sometimes they are students with diagnosed disabilities who will need to learn coping skills other students may not need; but often these are students who have simply avoided reading and have at some point convinced themselves they will never be competent readers. My job becomes changing their minds.

I make sure I have books with a range of reading levels in every basket to be previewed, so if a student rates every book as too easy or too hard, it's a red flag to me that I'll need to confer with the student to unearth why he didn't find a single book at his reading level. Somewhere in every basket should be at least one book just right for each student. However, only deskside conferences can help me determine if a student's rating of books was accurate.

Assessing the reading level column of the Book Shopping Record Sheet helps me know:

- which students may be below-level readers and will need frequent conferences to spur their growth

- which students take the time to thoughtfully consider the readability level of a book before choosing it to read, as evidenced by a variety of responses in the reading level column of the record sheet.

- how much work I will have to do both with the class as a whole and with individual students to help develop strategies for approaching unknown words.

I repeat the book shopping process several times throughout the year. Any time I see student enthusiasm waning, I grab books from the classroom and school libraries and we spend a day shopping again. By this time, my students know they will be spending thirty minutes a day reading, so this gives them another chance to find some books they will actually want to read.

Book Shopping Record Sheets give me a snapshot of where students are as readers. The picture will become clearer as I work side-by-side with these students in conferences throughout the year.

The Benefit of Time Well Spent

While these initial lessons consume the first two to three weeks of the school year, they are an essential key to student engagement. When students have had a chance to write down titles of books they would actually like to read, they become motivated to choose their own books and to do so with success. By showcasing the various types of books available to them, clarifying what to expect from each type of book, and giving students chances to actually explore the books themselves, I have created a culture of excitement centered around reading. Jobe and Dayton-Sakari (1999) remind teachers, "Choice is power. In a literacy interaction, whoever picks what to read holds the power and the other person is just along for the ride" (35). Teachers should strive to put their students in the driver's seat—not just for a day, but for a lifetime.

Making Good Choices in the Library

After the levees in New Orleans collapsed in the wake of Hurricane Katrina, many survivors evacuated to Houston. The intermediate school where I was teaching was privileged to welcome almost 100 of these students. They were traumatized and saddened by their ordeal, but they and their families were grateful for the education the students were receiving from their first day with us.

A few weeks after the students arrived, one of my teachers was called to the office and greeted by a furious mother. "Go ahead," she said, nudging her daughter. "Show it to her and tell her what you did."

Sheepishly, the girl pulled a library book out of her backpack. "See," the mother stormed, "she stole this book from the school. I'm not raising my daughter to be a thief."

The book in question was a library book. Neither the girl nor her mother had ever been in a school with a library where they could check books out to take them home. I suddenly realized how many things I often take for granted.

I cannot assume that trips to the library will always be productive. Students who have had very little experience in libraries are not the only ones who will need support in selecting books. Even gifted readers sometimes have no idea how books are arranged or find the Dewey decimal system to be intimidating, hesitating to ask for help out of embarrassment. Many readers may stick to one genre solely because they're too afraid to wander and browse in an unfamiliar section of the library. And far too many students may consider library time only a chance to socialize with their friends. Changing student expectations for time in the library is an important first step toward increasing students' engagement with texts.

Teaching a Reader's Expectations for Books

I make clear to my students that their job in the library is to choose books they intend to read all the way through. If students are never actually expected to finish the books they choose, is it any wonder that they develop such cavalier attitudes toward reading?

I often visit classrooms before the first trip to the library each year to do a series of lessons on expectations. On the first day, I always ask, "What is your job when you go to the library?"

The students always answer, "To get a book."

"What kind of book?" I ask.

At this point, the students always look at me with incredulous stares. I know that in their heads they are thinking, What is wrong with this woman? We just told her we go there to get a book. What does she mean what *kind* of book? A *library* book, of course.

When I ask this question, I look for a specific answer. I want students to know that when they go to the library their job is to find a book they will *understand*, *finish*, and *enjoy*. They must learn to choose books for independent reading that are both at the correct level and interesting to them. Otherwise, students who are below-level readers will not be likely to spend the extra time it will take for them to reach grade-level expectations.

Before going to the library, I offer explicit instruction on its organization and on the information found on the spines of library books. **Students must understand that:**

- Fiction is in a separate section from nonfiction.

- Fiction titles are arranged alphabetically by the author's last name, so they must know that name.

- Biographies are arranged alphabetically by the subject's last name, not the author's.

- Nonfiction is arranged numerically.

- The nonfiction numbers have meaning.

- The letters and numbers on the spines of books are there to help us find them easily in the library.

I make sure my students know these things because I have learned I truly cannot take anything for granted.

Easing the Hunt for Books

It is one thing for students to know what kind of book they want to find—and quite another to actually locate it in the vast wasteland of bookshelves that is alien territory to far too many. It is not enough for me to teach my students how to choose books; I also have to be sure they know how to find them in the library.

On the first day my class is going to the school library to check out books, I stand at the front of the room and ask a simple question: "How do you find a book you want to read in the library?"

Hands go up around the room, and I call on a student. "You go to the card catalog," he replies.

"Yes, you do! Good job. Now who can explain to me how to *use* the card catalog?"

After a great deal of wait time, another student suggests, "You type in the kind of book you want and it tells you where to find it."

"But what do I type in?" I ask. This is my chance to provide an on-the-spot minilesson that will let my students know that the card catalog can be sorted three ways—by title, by subject, or by author. I want them to understand that readers who plan to finish and enjoy the books they choose have a purpose when they go to the card catalog—they are going to find another book written by an author they enjoy, a specific book they've heard about from another reader, or a book in a genre or about a topic in which they already know they are interested. They need to know that sitting in front of a computerized card catalog is not a technology exercise—it is a step in finding the next best book they've ever read.

Other responses from the class can prompt other quick minilessons (Figure 3–9), all designed to guarantee better book choices once we get to the library. These choices will determine how quickly supported independent reading begins to spur student growth in my classroom.

◎ Dealing with Poor Choices

No matter how much time I spend teaching students to make good choices, some will still choose poorly. They are either not yet committed to finding books they will enjoy or they still don't understand how to do it. These poor choices cannot be ignored—they have to be addressed.

How Do You Choose a Book in the Library?

Student Suggestion	Follow-Up Question	On-the-Spot Minilesson
I just go find the one I want.	Who can tell me how to decide what kind of book I want?	Readers use what they already know to help them find books to read; they look for authors they like, series they enjoy, books other people have recommended, or books about subjects they're interested in.
I go to the shelves and find one I like.	Who can tell me how you know which shelf to go to in the library?	The library has three sections: the fiction section, the nonfiction section, and the reference section.
I go to the card catalog.	Who can tell me how to use the card catalog?	Card catalogs are library tools that help us find the books we are looking for.
I type in the kind of book I want.	Who can tell me how to decide what to type in the search area of the card catalog?	Card catalogs can be sorted by author, title, or subject. Readers think about these things when choosing a book.
I ask the librarian to help me find a good book.	Who can tell me what kind of question they might ask the librarian?	Readers ask librarians for specific help by already knowing what kind of book they might want and asking for suggestions or help in finding it in the library.
I just start looking at the books until I find one I like.	Who can tell me what to do when I'm standing in front of a bookshelf so that I can find a book I like?	Readers preview books by looking at the cover and reading the summaries on the back or on the front flyleaf.

Figure 3–9   *Sample Follow-Up Questions and Minilessons to Support Student Choice*

Library time for my students is not free time for me. This is not the time for me to run to the restroom, make a quick phone call, or chat with the librarian; this is the time to offer guidance when it is needed most—while students are actually trying to choose the books they will finish and enjoy.

Likewise, library time is not a social hour for students. Before ever leaving the classroom, I make my expectations clear: students will be actively looking for books to read and will speak only to adults who can help them locate titles they might enjoy. I also have students write three ideas for books on slips of paper before they ever leave the classroom so that I can see they are putting thought into their choices. This gives them a chance to ask their classmates the titles or authors of books they might like to read so that these conversations aren't necessary once they get to the library. One of the best teachers I know stands by the checkout counter in the library and personally inspects every book students are planning to check out. If they have not made good reading choices, she accompanies them back to the shelves to choose again.

I believe students should always read in self-selected texts during supported independent reading time. But for students who are overwhelmed by the amount of books available to them, I often offer five or six suggestions. I actually put the book choices in the students' hands if at all possible. If they still have trouble choosing, I might narrow the choices even further or ask them to tell me what they'd like to have in a book that none of my choices has offered—and then I get some more choices for them to preview. I try *never* to choose a book for a student—but I will break even that rule once in a great while if I think it is in the student's best interest. But I try every trick I know to get them into books more or less on their own before I step in and choose for them—and in a normal school year I can count on one hand the number of books I have chosen for students to read.

To ensure a more successful experience, I wait to take students to the library until I have invested time teaching them how to make good choices once they get there. **I need to be sure that the answers to all of these questions are *yes* before my students ever line up at the classroom door:**

- Do my students understand that they should choose a book they expect to finish and enjoy?

- Do they know that there are two sections in the library—fiction and nonfiction—and how to find a book in each one?

- Have I spent time showcasing both fiction and nonfiction books that may interest them?

- Have I given them time to talk to each other about books they have read and enjoyed?

- Do they know what a card catalog is and how to use it?

- Do they understand what the information on the spines of library books tells us?

- Do they know how to preview a book to see if they will like it?

- Have they *practiced* the five-finger-rule method of judging a book's readability?

- Do they know exactly what kind of book they are looking for before they ever leave the classroom?

By asking these questions beforehand and ensuring positive responses, I am arming my students with the knowledge they need to make good book choices for themselves.

◎ *Student Accountability*

Perhaps the most important expectation I can communicate to students in my independent reading classroom is that they should accept responsibility for their own reading development. Therefore, I will hold them accountable for choosing texts that will engage them. I can certainly steer them to books they might enjoy, but in the end, it is the students who must select the books they will read. If they don't like the books they have chosen, *they* should be held responsible for having made a bad choice. Students readily blame teachers when they don't like assigned reading; they have only themselves to blame when they are not enjoying books they have self-selected. They will need my support and guidance to realize that the freedom to choose comes with a responsibility to choose well.

I will also hold them accountable for actually finishing books. Disengaged readers often jump from book to book, never finding one that they actually intend to read all the way through. For them, choosing a book is just going through the motions of doing something for me, not something for themselves as readers. Even though in real life it's okay to abandon a book that isn't engaging us, in the classroom I try to stick to the message that readers finish books—and students in my reading classroom should be expected to do so as well.

I expect students to use supported independent reading time to actually read. I nudge them to have books out ready to read each day when reading time begins—and they learn that any off-task behavior gets addressed in a deskside conference. They learn that I won't let them abuse the time I have given them to develop as readers.

Because reading is an internal process, we teachers have to have some way of assessing the quality of our students' reading experience. Students' maintenance of personal anchor charts (Chapter 4), reading logs (Chapter 10), and reading responses (Chapter 4) are requirements—not options. I stubbornly insist that all students complete these brief assignments every day—and I check to be sure they do so. (See Chapter 10 for more on assessment.)

Most important, I expect students to continue to grow as readers. They have to be willing to place themselves in a state of disequilibrium (Caine and Caine 1994). There will be confusion as texts present ideas that challenge what the readers thought they knew—and the students must be motivated to do the work necessary to eliminate this confusion. The continual resolution of these conflicts restructures the brain and makes it capable of more sophisticated thinking. So, my students must be committed to opening themselves up to uncertainty, all the time believing that with my support they can meet the challenges necessary to grow.

If I want my students to be risk takers who will become increasingly more engaged and proficient readers, I have to model what it is to be open to new challenges rather than afraid of them or turned off by them. One powerful way to create this culture is to nurture the relationships that exist between all the readers in the classroom, including myself. And, above all, I must give my students ample opportunity to discover that they control their own reading destinies.

Questions for Reflection

Readers know how to choose books that they will understand and enjoy. As you think about helping your students develop this important skill, consider these questions:

- Do you spend time showcasing enticing books so they will know what they actually want to read?

- Do you take the time before going to the library to make sure every student has a plan for finding a book after you get there?

- Do you regularly talk to your school librarian and other experts about what books and authors are most popular in your building, both fiction and nonfiction?

- Do you regularly read reviews of children's and young adult literature and search websites so that you will know what books you can recommend?

- Do you bring in book reviews that have compelled you to read a new book, so that students see how you find out about great new books?

- Do you read the books your students are reading so you can become part of their reading community?

Time spent exposing students to a variety of engaging texts is time spent ensuring that an independent reading classroom is time students spend growing as readers.

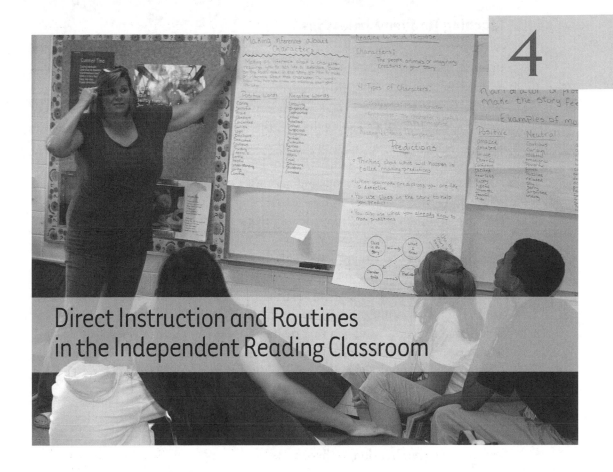

4

Direct Instruction and Routines in the Independent Reading Classroom

One afternoon, I sat in a meeting with a group of young social studies teachers as they wrestled with ideas to make their instruction more effective. This is an incredibly energetic group of young people who love both their content and their students, but the recent benchmark test they had given had revealed a true cause for concern: only 42 percent of their students had passed. Something needed to change.

"I've been trying to keep my lessons shorter," Chelsea said. "I really think I've been talking too much. I'm trying not to talk longer than fifteen minutes every period now."

After several minutes of kicking this idea around, one of the other teachers said, "Where'd you get this idea?"

"It's what they do in language arts," she answered.

Teaching Through Minilessons

Limiting direct instruction to fifteen minutes is certainly what the language arts teachers in my building try to do. Instructional minutes are precious—and as the managers of those minutes, we need to make good decisions about how they are spent. It is very easy to spend more time talking than we think we do, to jump in and talk when our students don't respond to a question right away rather than waiting for them to find answers themselves. Author and educator Linda Hoyt recently told our district literacy coaches that *she* is now keeping her direct instruction to no more than fifteen minutes (Hoyt 2008). She says she carries a timer and when it goes off, she quits teaching and puts the kids to work—no matter what. Her contention is that kids should spend at least forty-five of every sixty minutes engaged in *authentic* (emphasis mine) reading and writing activities rather than in teacher-centered instruction.

In order to give students the time they need to read, I have had to learn to teach in short, focused bursts of instruction known as *minilessons*. Minilessons are a chance to remind students *how* and *why* people read. They are an opportunity to make clear to students that reading is not moving our eyes across a string of letters; reading is thinking about the words on the page. These quick reminders before reading should be short, sweet, and to the point. **Minilessons should focus on one of three key areas:**

- students' engagement with texts

- their comprehension of these texts

- their individual growth as readers.

Breaking Down a Complex Task: Three Types of Knowledge

Reading is a bit like spinning plates. Proficient readers do countless numbers of things all at the same time—and to an outsider it looks effortless. Effective teachers must take this complicated process and break it into small, manageable chunks—and find ways to present these chunks to students so that the effect on their reading will be immediate.

Instruction in a reading classroom is seamless, moving smoothly from the minilesson to independent reading to the conference to the response. This requires a narrow focus and effective planning. Each element of the lesson must flow effortlessly into the next. The response is modeled in the minilesson and the focus of that minilesson becomes the basis for the questions that start deskside conferences. Meanwhile, students immediately apply the skill or strategy during their independent reading time and make their thinking visible through reading responses.

Students will not retain a concept if too much information is given in a single shot. I spend time retracing my own thinking as a proficient user of the targeted skill or strategy, focusing on every single step in its effective application. Then I teach those steps one at a time so that my students, too, can apply the strategy as experts. **When I begin to plan a series of lessons on a skill or strategy, I consider three questions:**

- What exactly is it I'm teaching—and how would I define it to the students? (declarative knowledge)

- What are the steps I use in applying this skill or strategy to my reading? (procedural knowledge)

- When do I use this particular strategy or skill—and how does it help me as a reader? (conditional knowledge)

Let's say I am planning a series of lessons on inferences. First, my students will need to know that an inference is an educated guess that combines ideas from the text with what they personally know about the world to create an idea that is written between the lines. This is declarative knowledge. Then they have to learn how to gather clues from a text and read through and past them to get the author's meaning. This is procedural knowledge. And then they must develop the conditional knowledge to know that readers expect to infer all the time; they understand it is part of the interaction between authors and the people who have chosen to read what they have written. Without this interaction people merely *decode* words, not *read* them.

If students are to truly grasp the idea of inferences, the teaching can't stop at declarative knowledge. It has to move deeper into the realms of procedural and conditional knowledge—and this knowledge must be immediately applied to the texts these students have chosen to read.

Anchoring the Lesson in Common Texts

Once the knowledge about the skill or strategy has been determined, the next step is situating its use in an authentic text that will serve as a vehicle for modeling and provide a common reading experience for a very diverse classroom of readers. An anchor text becomes a reference to which I can later point when asking students to independently use the skills, strategies, and modes of thinking modeled during this shared experience. When I center my teaching around an authentic short text read aloud to students, the students not only gain knowledge of the habits of avid readers but also a hunger for texts that will engage them and offer multiple opportunities for rich discussions with other readers.

Anchor texts need to offer an obvious opportunity to apply the skill or strategy that is the lesson's target. Picture books, short stories, newspaper and magazine articles, poetry, and excerpts from longer texts all work well. I use excerpts more often than not. Besides serving as a vehicle for modeling, a well-chosen excerpt will stir students' interest in the longer book.

For my lesson on inferring, I choose an excerpt from the beginning of the book *The Adoration of Jenna Fox* (Pearson 2008). It is a fairly new book, and most students will be unfamiliar with it. The book begins,

> I used to be someone.
>> Someone named Jenna Fox.
>> That's what they tell me. But I am more than a name. More than they tell me. More than the facts and statistics they fill me with. More than the video clips they make me watch.
>> More. But I'm not sure what.
>> "Jenna, come sit over here. You don't want to miss this." The woman I am supposed to call Mother pats the cushion next to her. "Come," she says again.
>> I do. (3)

There are ample opportunities in this short text to collect clues and make inferences in fifteen minutes or less. In addition, this opening is intriguing enough to generate interest in the book itself. This makes it a good choice for my minilesson.

Using Anchor Charts to Hold Shared Thinking

As I model my thinking using authentic texts, I simultaneously create an anchor chart based on the key points of the lesson. The purpose of an anchor is to hold something in place. Anchor charts, then, hold the key elements of instruction in place while students work to internalize what has been taught.

Whenever possible, I use graphic organizers to anchor the learning presented in a minilesson. Students copy these organizers into their reader's notebooks as we work through the anchor text together. This not only keeps every student actively involved during the lesson but also provides students with a readily available reference to help them as they read. Later, students can add their own examples to these charts as a response to their independent reading. Students are then in control of their own learning.

These notebooks can be spiral-bound with a section left blank for charts, though I prefer having students keep them in some kind of loose-leaf notebook so they can continually build their references. Folders with brads work well, as do small vinyl notebooks. Larger notebooks are fine if there is room to store them. I never let these notebooks leave the room because they may never find their way back, so the amount of space available in the classroom for storage should be considered. These notebooks combined with the class anchor charts become our textbook.

I don't draw anchor charts on transparencies because transparencies are only visible when I choose them to be. I want the students to be able to access this information any time they need it as readers, so I create the charts on butcher or chart paper, which can be displayed in the room at all times.

When I teach more than one group of students a day, I create a new chart for each class. Putting up a chart made earlier in the day is not as effective as building a chart with the students sitting in the room. At the end of the day, I choose one to post in the room or create a new one that compiles all the information collected across the various classes. As the year progresses, old charts will need to make way for new ones. I place the charts that are removed on a flip chart to which the students and I can return as needed.

Anchor Charts in Action: Lesson on Inferences

For my lesson on inferences, I use a T-chart as an anchor. I label the left column *Details from the Text* and the right column *Inference* (Figure 4–1). The position of the columns is intentional; readers must collect evidence *before* they use these details as a basis for inferring.

I include the title and author of the anchor text on the chart so that students will remember it when I refer to it in conferences or minilessons later. It also reminds them of books that caught their attention and that they might want to read.

"I found a great new book," I begin. "It's called *The Adoration of Jenna Fox* by Mary E. Pearson. As a reader, I know that as I read I will always need to make inferences [conditional knowledge]. Inferences are guesses based on the information the author has given me in the text [declarative knowledge]. It's sort of like a game. The author gives me clues and I use what I know about the world to put them together and figure out what she's trying to tell me [procedural knowledge].

"At the beginning of a fiction book, I know that I am going to have to make inferences about the characters and the setting. So as I start to read this book I

Inferences We Made

Anchor Text: *The Adoration of Jenna Fox* by Mary E. Pearson

Details from the Text	Inference
Jenna is not sure who she is.*	
People told her her name.*	
Somebody is filling her with facts.*	
She is being made to watch video clips.*	Jenna must have amnesia.
She is supposed to call some woman Mother.*	
She does what the woman tells her to.	

Figure 4–1   *Sample Anchor Chart*

am looking for the clues the author has left and using them to figure out what's going on in the story. Today I'd like to have you help me do that.

"Take out your reader's notebooks and let's create an anchor chart for inferences. It will be a two-column chart, so draw a line down the middle of the page. On the left-hand side write *Details from the Text*. This is where we're going to put the clues from the text. On the right-hand side write *Inference*. That's where we'll make our guesses. Remember to put the author and title of this anchor text at the top of the page.

"I'm going to read the first six paragraphs to you just so you can hear what they're about. Then I'll put the text on the board and we'll start gathering clues."

After reading the text aloud, I put a copy on the document reader or overhead projector. Then I tell the class, "Inferences are based on details in the text. What details has Mary Pearson given us about Jenna in these first six paragraphs?"

As students identify the details, I highlight them in the text and post them on the anchor chart. Then I move to the next piece of procedural knowledge.

"Now that I have collected these details, I need to connect them to what I already know about the world. Based on the evidence we have here, what inference can we make about Jenna?"

When the students infer that Jenna has amnesia, I tell them, "Let's put an asterisk by the details that would prove that Jenna has lost her memory." Then one by one we go down the list, starring clues that support that inference.

When we finish the list, there is a detail left over: Jenna does what her "mother" tells her to. "Hmmm," I say, "what do we do with this detail?" As students throw out ideas of what this clue could mean, I have a chance to stress the importance of solid evidence to support their inferences. When a student suggests Jenna is afraid of her mother, I say, "Is there enough evidence yet for me to prove that?" The answer of course is no. This gives me a chance to talk about predictions, which are a type of inference. I say, "When we *think* something *might* be true, we can make that into a question that we'll try to prove as we keep reading. The question *Is Jenna afraid of her mom?* will push us ahead as readers."

"Now, remember," I caution, "to make an inference you need more than one detail to support it. Keep reading and collecting until you're sure it's true. Until then, it's a prediction—and a question that keeps you moving forward."

Near the front of the room, I post a chart with a list of all the skills and strategies studied as a class in the order in which we studied them (Figure 4–2). At the end of the minilesson, I ask the class to summarize what we have learned and add

---

Skills and Strategies for Readers

Readers . . .

1. use the words the author gives to create images in their minds.

2. make connections between what the author has written and their own experiences.

3. use the meanings of prefixes and suffixes as clues to the meaning of unknown words.

4. expect to be at least a little confused at the beginning of a book.

5. use questions to drive the reading forward.

6. look for information about characters, setting, and problem at the beginning of a book.

7. notice clues about a story's time and place (setting).

8. think about how the setting affects what happens in the story.

9. collect clues about characters and use them to determine character traits.

10. notice how a character's traits affect what happens in the story.

11. think about what it is the character wants and identify what stands in his or her way (the problem)

12. make inferences by connecting details in the text to what they know about the world.

Figure 4–2 *Skills and Strategies Anchor Chart*

that to the chart. For the lesson on inferences, we add: Readers make inferences by connecting details in the text to what they know about the world. If I am spending several days on one skill or strategy, these statements become a convenient way to start the review lesson in the days that follow.

The lessons are numbered on the chart to serve as a table of contents for student notebooks. This list is cumulative and visible all year as a record of what has been learned. It provides a quick reference point when reminding students of the habits of skilled readers.

Reading Responses That Link Instruction and Practice

As I've said, I have students complete a response based on their independent reading every day. These responses make a reader's thinking visible. They are one of the tools I use to assess the progress of individual readers (see Chapter 10)— but they will be ineffective unless they benefit the students as well.

Effective responses have four characteristics. They

1. target an essential skill or strategy that was reviewed in the minilesson

2. facilitate rather than limit students' comprehension

3. can be completed in approximately five minutes

4. enhance rather than interrupt the reading experience.

Well-designed responses benefit both the students and the teacher. By holding the focus of the response in their minds as they read, my students are practicing the invisible habits of skilled readers. By analyzing graphic organizers that take very little time to check, I learn how well my students have mastered these skills and can prepare to move in with more support for the students who will need it. A carefully planned organizer becomes more than a way to hold students accountable for their reading. It becomes a vehicle for extending their thinking.

As I end my minilesson on inferring, I tell the students, "Today while you're reading I want you to collect details from the text that you can use to make inferences. At the end of reading time, you'll use those details to make inferences. Remember to write these details in your own words on the anchor charts you've already created and to write the title and author of *your* book underneath what we did together today. After you have listed the details on your chart, you can make inferences and put asterisks by the statements that prove them true.

"I'll bring each of you some little sticky notes in case you just want to mark the clues as you read rather than stopping to write them down. You can always write them down at the end of reading time."

This minilesson ties the direct instruction to the readers' responses and gives me a starting point for deskside conferences. It provides focused instruction, followed by immediate application of what has been taught to the students' own real reading. This is the way I help my readers grow.

Teaching the Routine of Supported Independent Reading Time

Once the minilesson ends each day, supported independent reading time begins. This is the students' chance to apply what I have just taught in a meaningful way. My role during this critical time is to check in with readers as they work on their own and to support them when I uncover areas of confusion. Individual readers may need help not only with skills and strategies that have been studied by the whole class, but also with challenges they encounter on their own that may not have been addressed in other instruction. Sometimes I will identify these areas for growth, and sometimes the focus of a deskside conference will be determined by the questions the readers have.

My expectations for students during supported independent reading time are simple:

- Have a book on your desk ready to read when reading time begins.

- Log in on your reading log before you begin reading.

- Read for the entire thirty minutes.

- Log out on your reading log and complete your response assignment.

These expectations are posted at the front of the room—but I have to teach them too.

When I work with new teachers as they learn to set up their classrooms and write their lesson plans, my advice is always this: Picture what would happen if everything went wrong—and teach to avoid that chaos. Veteran teachers all agree that time spent teaching expectations and routines is time well spent.

The first expectation for independent reading time that I teach is that the books the students read will be at their desks *before* independent reading time arrives. Chaos will ensue if students do not have books to read during this critical time. They can find countless ways to waste an entire thirty minutes finding a book to read. They give all kinds of reasons for why they don't have one—they left the book at home, they left it in their locker, they lost it, they finished it, they didn't like it. But whatever the reason, they don't have anything to read—so reading time will be totally wasted.

Students should know from the beginning that the books in the classroom library are not decorations   they are sweet temptations meant to whet their appetites for reading. I encourage them to look at these books at every appropriate time. Appropriate times could include when they first arrive in the classroom, when they have finished their classwork and asked permission to visit the library, or before or after school with teacher permission and a pass. Students should *not* be crowded around the shelves during independent reading time. Time spent at the shelves is time that is *not* spent reading.

Students know when they are nearing the end of a book—and I teach them that readers already know what they are going to read next. They should have the next book picked out and at their desk before they ever read that final word. Students also know when they have forgotten their book at home, and I expect them to choose a new book from the classroom library before reading time begins.

If I want my students to be readers, I have to teach them to think like readers. Readers never go anywhere without a book. They have two or three in a bag for long airplane trips in case they finish one of them. They have books on their desks at work, books at home, and books in the car. They want to be able to read every chance they get—and I want my students to learn these same habits.

In intermediate classrooms, students can keep books in their desks or tote trays ready to read. In middle school classrooms, students can tag books with sticky notes and leave them on a table or the teacher's desk so that if they arrive without a book one will be available when reading time begins. If I require that every student has a book ready to read at the beginning of independent reading time and enforce that expectation, it will become a habit for my students.

Early in the year I keep a stack of books on my desk—fiction and nonfiction books at various reading levels. If a student does not have a book to read, I choose three or four books from the stack, place them on the student's desk, and expect one to be chosen for reading. As I get to know my students better, I can predict which students won't have books—and I will be ready, armed before they arrive with several titles I have chosen just for them that are at the right reading level and should be of interest. I will allow them to choose the one they will read—but it will *not* involve standing at the shelves in the classroom library.

My students need to know that I expect them to read the entire thirty minutes. Reading does not mean writing or talking or staring into space—reading means reading. Early in the year a lot of conference time will be spent redirecting disengaged readers—but my persistence will pay off. In time, my students will believe that they are expected to spend independent reading time actually reading.

The Difference Seamless Instruction Can Make

Several years ago a teacher who was experimenting with supported independent reading came to me with a genuine concern. "I still feel like there must be something I'm missing. My kids are reading and I'm trying to do deskside conferences during that time, but I'm never sure what to ask when I talk to them—and I'm not sure they're learning anything."

"Have you checked their responses to see if they understood what you taught that day?"

"Well, actually, I don't usually have them do responses. They just read and visit with me in conferences."

"When you're conferring with them, do you ask questions about what you focused on in your minilesson?"

"Well, no, they've already done a worksheet or read something quick and written about it before we go to reading time. I check those to see if they got the lesson. So when I confer with them, I usually ask them to tell me what's going on in their book."

This teacher was moving in the right direction. My suggestion to her was that she try modeling a response during her minilesson, having the students replicate that response using their self-selected text, and asking students questions based on that minilesson during conferences to see if they were able to apply what she had taught.

A week later the teacher called me on the phone. "You were right!" she cheered. "I tried what you said and it worked. My conferences are so much stronger—and I know the kids are getting it. Thank you, thank you, thank you."

This teacher had learned the power of instruction that links to both students' responses and deskside conferences. Her students will be the ones issuing thanks in the end.

Questions for Reflection

Effective instruction is critical in any classroom. If you want to maximize the impact of your lessons, consider these questions:

- Did you think through the declarative, procedural, and conditional knowledge students need to successfully utilize the skill or strategy on which you are focusing?

- Are you consciously trying to focus your lessons so tightly that you can teach them in fifteen minutes or less?

- Are you matching texts to your instruction rather than starting your planning with texts?

- Have you modeled all the steps you will ask your students to take and created charts they can use as models as they work independently on this skill or strategy?

- Have you made sure that every student has a text with which they can appropriately practice the targeted skills and strategies?

If you can begin to deliver focused, seamless instruction, you will maximize your students' growth as independent readers.

5

Teaching Through Deskside Conferences

In response to Texas' policy of retaining fifth graders who do not pass our state's reading assessment, the intermediate school where I worked decided to create an intervention team. We chose two of our strongest teachers to work with students who had failed the state tests in fourth grade. Each teacher taught two groups of students, one in the morning and another in the afternoon. We put students who had failed reading in the language arts teacher's morning group and those who had failed math with the math teacher. Then the math coach and I went in every morning to work with these below-level students.

At the start of the year, Mikaela VandeWater, the language arts teacher on the team, and I each taught guided reading groups during the time I was with her. Students who were not in one of our groups were "independently reading." But as I looked out in the room I noticed that most of them were *not* reading. At best, they were only pretending. Here was a group of kids who needed to consume vast amounts of words to catch up with their same-age peers—and we were wasting at least thirty minutes of their time every day.

As a secondary-certified teacher, I embraced a workshop model back in the 1990s and never looked back. I was uncomfortable, however, with the workshop tenet that the teacher reads while the students are reading. I felt like I was missing countless teachable moments. So, one day I got up and starting conferring with my students. This shift in my teaching changed everything for me and my middle school students, so I felt confident it could change these fifth-grade readers as well. One day I suggested that instead of meeting with a small group, I would confer with the students who were not with Mikaela as they read in their independent reading books. Since I spent an hour in the class every day, every student could be supported during independent reading because Mikaela's small groups never lasted more than thirty minutes.

Mikaela began each day with a minilesson that targeted specific skills and strategies from the curriculum. Then she chose groups of four to six students to meet with her in a guided reading setting to continue work on these skills or to review something with which they had struggled in previous lessons. While she taught these small-group lessons, I conferred with students who were reading in their independent reading books, basing my initial questions on the content that had been covered that day and fitting my individual instruction to the needs of the students. I spent sixty minutes every day helping student readers.

With the new model in place, we began to see incredible growth in the students. By midyear, the morning group—the kids who had failed the reading test—were outperforming the afternoon group—the kids who had failed only math. We saw that same progress for the remainder of the year, and our state test verified it. As powerful as guided reading is, I truly believe that supported independent reading for students in intermediate and secondary grades is even stronger. Deskside conferences were at the center of this success.

Deskside Conferences as Vehicles for Teaching

Deskside conferences are conversations between a teacher and a student that serve two purposes: they build a relationship between teacher and student and provide direction to help the student grow as a reader. They begin as soon as the minilesson ends. These conferences are the most important and effective teaching I do in the course of a day.

Deskside conferences are teacher initiated but student driven. They take place wherever students are reading—which may be on the floor or in the hallway rather than at a desk. Although I may plan a focus for the conferences before I begin them or plan which students I want to see each day, these plans are always subject to change—and change is the one constant during conference time.

I approach a deskside conference the same way my doctor approaches her visits with me. I focus for a period of time on one reader and one reader only, analyzing that reader's needs at the moment and sifting through my bank of knowledge about reading to provide exactly the right "cure" for the problem of the moment. If I'm lucky, the reader is sailing along just fine and needs only a quick checkup. But if a student *is* in need of intervention, I can prescribe the right cure if I ask the right questions and quickly analyze the student's response.

I conduct the majority of my conferences on my knees. To stand above a student while conferring conveys a sense of control. There should be no control issue in a conference—it is simply a two-way conversation. The student and I need to be on equal footing so there is no power struggle involved.

The time spent conferring with a student is sacred. During that slice of time, my attention is on that student and that student only. I make my expectations clear: each student must honor the time I am giving to another member of their community during a conference. With time, the students understand that their turn with me will come and they, too, will receive my undivided attention.

Unlike the conferences that occur in lower grades that often focus on issues of decoding and fluency (Calkins 2001), conferences in the intermediate grades and middle school focus on comprehension and strategies. It is important when students are reading independently that they read in books that do *not* require them to continually face decoding challenges. With the wide variety of books available at the reading levels of even the lowest intermediate and middle school students, it is possible for every student in the room to find a readable text whose original purpose was to involve readers in a good story or to help them learn about a topic of interest to them. It is critical that the main focus with independent readers be on comprehension.

The Purpose and Structure of a Conference

A deskside conference is a way to assess the reading health of students in the classroom and provide targeted instruction at the point of need. It is a way of supporting students as they work in their individual zones of proximal development

(Vygotsky 1978). The purpose of a conference is always to push students to greater levels of reading proficiency.

The conference generally has five parts:

- the initial question

- analysis of the student's response

- the focusing comment

- the guiding advice

- the check for understanding

Preparing for the Conference

I need four things to begin a conference, three of which can be purchased at any office supply store: a clipboard, address labels or some other paper on which to take notes, and a pen or pencil. The fourth essential is a true desire to know students as readers coupled with a willingness to offer advice intended to help them grow.

I always plan to check with the students on the skills or strategies that have been targeted during instruction. Early in the year, the focus is on engagement. I check with students while they're reading to be sure they are involved in the texts they have chosen. Later, if I have taught a strategy such as making connections, the conversation could start with asking students to show a place where they made a connection and explain that connection to me. If the class has worked on a skill such as character analysis, the conference could start with me asking for a character sketch of the main character.

If the students can easily answer the questions I ask, they are clearly doing fine and don't need help that day, so I move on to the next reader. But these students cannot be abandoned—tomorrow might bring a true reading challenge for them. It is essential for me to touch base every few days even with the most capable readers—they aren't finished growing and they will need my care and support as well.

During the conference, my aim is to discover what challenges confront the individual readers in the room and to help them understand and overcome these challenges. I am constantly monitoring their engagement, their comprehension, and their growth. I am watching their application of the skills and strategies taught during direct instruction and asking focused questions to determine where their thinking has gone awry. As I conduct deskside conferences, I am both detective and teacher—uncovering clues to reading confusions and offering instruction that addresses the individual needs of each student in the room.

Initiating the Conference

Conferences begin with a question from the teacher to the student. The questions I use most often are:

- What are you reading today?

- Do you like your book so far?

- How's the reading going today?

- What's been happening so far in your book?

- What page are you on right now?

These simple questions are nonthreatening and open the door for further conversation. They temporarily take the reader's attention away from the text and focus it on what they are doing as readers.

These seemingly casual questions actually provide me with important information. I ask students who often change books what they are reading today to see if they have finally found a book that engages them. If not, the work today will be on engagement. If students who have had trouble finding a book to enjoy are reading for the second or third day in the same book, I ask what they like about the book so far to help me know what kinds of books they are enjoying so they can be steered to their next good read.

Asking how the reading is going today helps me see if my minilessons have helped or if students who have been reading right along have suddenly hit a snag, as can certainly happen in more sophisticated, longer texts. I ask students who have been having trouble comprehending or keeping a storyline in mind as they read through chapter books what's been happening in their books. Their answers will indicate if they need to go back and reread or if they're doing quite well. And for competent readers who speed through the world a book has created for them, as well as readers who are making such slow progress that I suspect that they might be in a book that's over their heads, I always ask, "What page are you on right now?"

Tone of voice is critical. My inflection should never give students a clue as to why the question is being asked. It is very tempting with students who have changed books five times in the last six days to say, "And what are you reading *today?*" but that clearly puts the student on the defensive from the beginning—and students won't learn if they are spending their time with an adversary for whom they feel they must provide a credible defense. In deskside conferences, a supportive tone is everything.

Focusing the Conference

I remember the first time I ever used a microscope. We were looking at drops of pond water to see in magnified horror all the tiny creatures that inhabit that universe—and my science lab partner was oohing and aahing. I couldn't wait for my turn!

But when my turn came, I couldn't see a thing. I just couldn't get the hang of looking with one eye and focusing the scope so I could actually see. What a disappointment—the rest of my sixth-grade class now realized whose territory we were invading each time we swam in a pond—but my lack of focus kept me in the dark.

Students' vision of reading shouldn't be blurred. For a conference to be successful, it is not enough for *teachers* to understand what they are hoping to accomplish that day. It needs to be a shared vision that both the student and teacher agree will be beneficial for that reader. If only *the teacher's* focus is clear, the conference will be a failure.

In the seconds after the student responds to the initial question, I must quickly decide what the focus will be for the conference that day. Often I have an idea in mind before stopping at the student's desk because I have reviewed my previous notes and have an idea where that student may be struggling. Sometimes, I plan to spend the day assessing individual students' understanding of the important skills or strategies I have been teaching during the minilessons. But in the end, it will be each student's response to the very first question that sets the direction—and the length—of the conference.

Once the focus for the intervention has been determined, I clearly state that focus to the student. I need to name the problem I've detected and what type of advice I plan to offer. I also have to remember that students bring strengths to their reading every day—and they will develop more quickly if the tools they have already mastered are continually celebrated.

For students who are having trouble finding books that capture their attention, the effort they've made in choosing the book they're holding should always be honored. If their response to a question about enjoying the book they have is lukewarm or negative, I might say, "I see you've picked an adventure book. Those books are always fun to read. Let's talk about what you can expect to find at the beginning of an adventure book." This honors the student's choice, makes an assumption about why engagement may not have occurred as yet, and states what help I am planning to offer that day.

For students who continue to read comfortable texts, it is good to cut a deal. After asking what they're reading, I might say, "You have really been enjoying these Amber Brown books. I think you've read about three of them so far, haven't you? I really like them, too—because Amber is *funny*! I don't want you to give up reading these books, but I'd like you to try reading some at a little bit higher level. You've improved so much as a reader that I think you're ready to try something different. Why don't you go ahead and finish this Amber Brown and I'll get some Melanie Martin and Ramona Quimby books for you to choose from for your next read? I think you'll like them—and I'll help you get started in one when the time comes."

The problem has been named—the book is not challenging enough—but the student's right to choose has been honored and she has been allowed to finish a book she will most likely enjoy. I have complimented her growth as a reader—and made a plan for what to read next. I must honor my promise and bring in some books from which she can choose. In addition, I must expect the student to honor her promise as well. She will need to actually read the book she chooses. I must be certain that any book I offer will be one the student is capable of reading—with support.

If a student's answer to "What's happening in your book so far?" is vague or clearly confused, I might say, "Why don't you read a little bit of the book to me?" I will be listening to see if the book is actually above the student's level and too much time is being spent dealing with unfamiliar words and sentence structures. If that is the case, I might say, "Boy, you really seem to be fighting with this text—that can't be much fun. Would you like to find another book that you might enjoy more? It's important to enjoy the time we spend reading."

I will ask the student what needs to be considered when the next book is chosen and what mistakes he made in choosing the current book. When he can identify what he needs to do differently this time to choose an appropriate text, I will send him to the school or classroom library or offer a stack of texts at the correct level for him to look through. I will allow him to abandon the initial book because students should never hate the time they spend reading—but the student must understand that he will be expected to finish the next book he chooses.

Sometimes asking students to just go back to the last point at which they understood what was going on is enough support, even if they go all the way back to page one. When asking students to find the last place where they were sure what was going on, I always ask them to summarize what happened up to that point and to read a page or two aloud. I listen carefully to the text and help the students notice the important information the author provided for the reader. If students don't seem to understand how I knew that would be important, it is time to explain that readers should go into fiction *expecting* to find out things about the setting, the characters, their problems, and the solutions, or into nonfiction *expecting* to learn something new. Readers must look for these things because no one can find what they're not looking for. Often this is enough to get a student going—but I will need to check back with the student every single day for a week or more to be certain that the text is manageable. (See Figure 5–1 for the most common problems and conference starters.)

Checking for Understanding

I never leave students until I am confident they understand what to do next. I restate what I have asked them to do and verify they know how this will help them as readers. If the student is not convinced the advice and guidance offered will help, I have just wasted everyone's time.

Students must find what I have asked them to do is valuable—or they will never do it. They must also believe they are capable of being competent readers. If my goal is to develop a lifelong love of reading in students, I have a professional responsibility to challenge developing readers' views of themselves as incompetent. They must learn to share the belief that they *can* comprehend and enjoy texts.

Keeping a Record of Deskside Conferences

An efficient note-taking system is an important element of planning and implementing good instruction. I have tried a number of systems—random notes on notebook paper that I later transcribed and transferred to folders, separate sheets of paper in a notebook for each student. Neither of these systems worked for me because they were too cumbersome. God bless the teacher I met in a workshop who suggested taking notes on address labels.

My procedure is simple. I place sheets of two-by-four-inch address labels from the local office supply store on a clipboard. On each label, I write a student's name so that there is a label for each student. This guarantees that I will confer with each student at some time over a three-day period.

Problem	Conference Starters
The student is not reading the same book she was reading the day before.	Can you help me understand why you changed books?
The student wants to abandon a book.	What mistakes did you make choosing this book—and how will you keep from making those same mistakes again?
The student is making extremely slow progress through a book.	• Why did you think this book would be interesting? • Would you read a little of this book to me?
The reader cannot summarize what has happened so far in the book.	• Can you show me the last place where you remember what you read? • Could you read a little of this book to me?
The reader does not understand how to carry information across from one chapter and day to the next.	• Can I show you a graphic organizer that might help you keep track of the important information in the book?
The student is unable to apply the skills and strategies taught in the minilesson to the text currently being read.	I'm going to read a section in your book and stop when I come to a part when I am [using whatever skill or strategy you have targeted]. Then I'm going to ask you to do the same thing.
The student is stuck in a genre or series.	I see you've really been enjoying [whatever kind of books]. Readers read from a lot of different kinds of books. What kind of book would you like to try next?
The book is too easy for the student.	I know you are really enjoying this book, and I'm glad. But because I want you to grow as a reader, I'd like you to try something a little harder next time. What do you think you might like to read?
The book is too hard for the student.	Would you please read a little bit of this book to me? You are spending a lot of time dealing with words you don't know—and that makes reading more work than pleasure. Let's see if we can find you a book that is more comfortable for you to read.
The student is confused about what is going on in the book.	Why don't you go back to the last place you understood what was happening? Readers reread when they're confused.

Figure 5–1   *The Most Common Focal Points for Conferences*

At the start of the conference, I write the day's date, the book the student is reading, and the page on which the student is working on the address label bearing that student's name. This helps me keep track of students who have changed books as well as those who are making good progress through the texts they have chosen.

I take notes on what has been discussed and on any action that needs to be taken before the student is seen again (Figure 5–2). If I am particularly concerned about a student, I will use a yellow highlighter to highlight the behavior I saw or the exact direction I have given to draw my attention to that student the next day as I begin my conferences. I will also review the labels at the start of each conference time to be certain that I touch base with students who have not had conferences in several days. Although these are probably the strongest readers in the room, they too deserve attention and instruction that will help them grow.

After a label has been filled with information, I peel it off the sheet of labels and move it to a sheet of paper with the student's name at the top. I keep these sheets in a notebook or in file folders so I can find them easily.

These notes become an ongoing record of each student's individual struggles and successes. They represent the individual assessment of student progress I conducted at every desk in the room during daily conference time. The gist of every conference is recorded here as is the frequency of the conferences. I can quickly remember what guiding advice I gave each student—and notice from my notes if that advice was helpful. I can watch students progress from challenged readers who must have my help to start each book to more independent readers who choose and start books on their own, recognizing when they need help and asking for it themselves. By reviewing everything written on these labels, I can assess student progress and plan future instruction. These individual sheets are invaluable when conducting parent conferences or meeting with other educators about students whose progress is an area of concern.

When I see a pattern of confusion in the classroom, I know I need to offer a minilesson on the common source of this confusion. If most students continue to struggle with a skill such as inferring, I will need to offer a series of minilessons on that skill, directly addressing the misunderstandings I have uncovered during conferences. If many students seem to be having trouble staying focused or want to abandon books, I will address those problems in a whole-group minilesson as well, offering advice on how to deal with distractions or reviewing one more time how to choose a book that will be finished and enjoyed.

By listening to students and working with them to help overcome any obstacles that keep them from truly loving the time they spend reading, I am reminded every day that there is a deep need in all of us to be good at the things that are important.

Aaron	Trisha
10/1—Reading Animorphs—*The Visitor*—p. 13 10/2—Same book. p. 15. Asked what was happening—seemed confused. Wasn't visualizing so didn't realize what had happened. Read aloud—he pictured and understood. Sticky to mark visualizations. 10/3—Had two stickies for images. Seems to be helping. p. 27. 10/4—p. 38 10/5—p. 50	10/1—Reading *Poppleton Has Fun*—has already finished *Poppleton*. 10/2—Reading another Poppleton book. Bring *Gooseberry Park*. 10/3—Loaned GP. 10/4—GP—p. 25.
Anh	**Jose**
10/1—Reading *Face on the Milk Carton* as part of book group—on Chapter 6 10/3—Chapter 8 10/5—Chapter 11	10/1—Reading *Stone Cold*—wrestling bio. Can only tell me what already knew. Is ignoring graphics. Asked to start over— list interesting new facts learned. 10/2—Recorded no facts yesterday. Started again. Took turns stopping when learned something new. Same assignment. 10/3—Still no new facts. Read one paragraph at time— stopped to retell. Is to have five facts by Friday. 10/4—Has two facts. Reminded of assignment. 10/5—Five facts.
Michael	**LaToya**
10/1—Reading *Face on the Milk Carton* as part of book group—on Chapter 5. 10/3—Chapter 6—Talked about being behind. Says likes book. Said would read extra time tonight to catch up. 10/4—Chapter 9—yeah!	10/2—Reading *Abby Hayes*—has read one before. Can name things she expects to see in the book. p. 27 10/3—p. 33 10/4—p. 48—named favorite part 10/5—p. 70

Figure 5–2 *Sample Conference Notes*

(Continued)

Kendrick	Lisa
10/2—Reading *Night of the Twisters*—seems disinterested. 10/3—Reading *Save Queen of Sheba*—can't retell. Didn't realize was historical fiction. Sent to classroom library for new book. Picked *Joey Pigza*. 10/4—Reading *Stone Cold* bio. Talked about abandoning books. Must finish book he is reading at end of period. Gave four choices. Talked about confusions at beginning of books—what to expect. 10/5—Began *Fried Worms*. Read aloud—I stopped him to have him notice characters, setting, and situation. p. 8.	10/2—Reading *Eragon*. Says she likes fantasy. Can tell me some characteristics of genre. p. 34. 10/5—*Eragon*—p. 107.
Leroy	**Malik**
10/3—Reading Goosebumps. Has read four others in series. p. 51. 10/4—p. 89 10/5—Finished Goosebumps. Recommended Wright or Hahn.	10/2—Reading *Face on the Milk Carton* as part of book group. On Chapter 7. Bought *Whatever Happened to Janie*. 10/4—Chapter 11

Figure 5–2 *(Continued)*

Reading is important—and no matter how much the students in any classroom try to deny it, they are deeply aware of its value. They want to be good readers—and I want that for them. Deskside conferences are a powerful way of helping me reach that goal—one day, one student, and one conquered obstacle at a time.

The Difference a Conference Can Make

Much to my amazement, Robert was actually reading that day—and had been reading every day that week. This was unusual behavior for him. He was repeating the grade and had always hated reading—independent reading time was usually the time he dreaded most in the day. But all this week he had been engrossed in an Animorphs book. Or so I thought.

Robert's teacher, one of the most skilled I know, had spent most of the last week teaching inferring, and the students were to be keeping track of their inferences as they read. During my conferences, I was going to see how the students were doing with this important skill.

I pulled up a chair next to Robert and said, "So, you're reading Animorphs, huh? Are you enjoying it?"

"Yeah, it's okay."

"I see you're on page 87," I noted as I wrote the book title and page number on an address label headed with his name. "Tell me what's been happening so far."

Robert explained that "some guy" was underground running. "Have you made any inferences so far?"

"Not really."

"You don't have any thoughts about what's about to happen? You said he's running?"

"Yeah."

Clearly we were getting nowhere, so I asked Robert to start reading to me. He was at a pivotal point in the plot when the protagonist was going to have to use his intelligence to help him escape. When Robert read that the hero felt a sharp tooth bite into his leg, I stopped him. "What do you think just happened?" I asked, trying to prompt an inference.

His eyes lit up. "A shark got him!" he exclaimed.

Not quite the answer I had in mind. Robert had just read three pages describing slithering creatures with sharp teeth that were chasing our brave hero through subway tunnels. The creatures' teeth had been described in horrifying detail. This should have been an easy inference to make. Where in the world did the sharks come from?

"Why do you think it's a shark?" I asked as Robert happily began to jot down his truly amazing inference.

"Because sharks have sharp teeth and it says right here that he felt a sharp tooth in his leg. Must have been a shark."

Needless to say, I spent a while with Robert that day. I explained that inferences are a junction between what is in the text and what is in our heads—but they must always start with the text. This text contained no sharks.

"But what else could have bitten his leg?" Robert asked.

I went back and reread the pages describing the creatures that were emerging from deep in the subway tunnel to devour everything in their path. When I finished all the specific description of horrific teeth one more time, I said, "Now do you know what bit him?"

"No."

"Robert," I said, "I'm going to read this one more time and I want you to use the words I read to make pictures in your head."

"What do you mean make pictures in my head?"

"You know, let the words help you call up images in your mind so you see what's happening in the book like a movie."

"You're kidding, aren't you?" he asked in amazement.

No, I most certainly was not. If I had waited to read Robert's page of inferences, I would never have realized that he not only did not understand that good inferences must be tied to information in the text but that he also did not ever make pictures in his head. This is especially significant when a student is reading science fiction, a genre that presents creatures and inventions that the reader has never really seen. Without the ability to visualize, science fiction can be almost incomprehensible.

That day Robert and I discussed three important things that he needed at exactly that moment: understanding the characteristics of the genre of science fiction, using words to make pictures in your head, and tying inferences to the text you are reading. Robert had been exposed to every idea we discussed multiple times in his school career and had not internalized any of it—but that day he actually *needed* these ideas to comprehend. We had just shared a classic "teachable moment." Had I been sitting down reading or working with a small group while Robert grappled with his Animorphs books, he might still believe a subway shark had attacked our brave hero. That is the difference supported independent reading can make.

Questions for Reflection

As you think about implementing deskside conferences in your classroom, here are some questions to consider:

- Have you explicitly taught your students the expectations you have for them to read the entire time?

- Have you decided how to keep anecdotal records on your daily conferences?

- Have you taught your students the importance of not interrupting a conference unless they are invited in?

- Are you prepared to offer minilessons to address the confusions your conferences uncover?

As you begin to experiment with deskside conferences, you will be amazed at what you will learn—not just about your students but about teaching reading as well. This learning will help both you and your students grow.

6

Capturing the Attention of Our Disengaged Readers

As reading teachers we have a lot on our plates. We sometimes get so caught up in the curriculum we are expected to cover and the demands of high-stakes testing that we forget that our students can't become better readers if they don't read. Even my best-laid plans can go awry. I can invest the time and money to create a reading culture in my classroom, offer lessons designed to engage students with texts, and give students chances to talk about these texts with other readers—yet still find there are students in the room who don't lose themselves in books because they have not chosen texts they truly intend to read or, even worse, don't understand the ones they've chosen. When dealing with students who are challenged in some way by the task of reading, it is nearly impossible to separate where engagement problems end and comprehension problems begin.

Some students actually choose books that initially excite them and therefore approach the reading ahead as an adventure. They are engaged as they begin reading—but as decoding issues, complications of plots, unfamiliar sentence structures, and other obstacles present themselves, they soon become frustrated and their engagement is shattered. They begin to look for ways to avoid reading, or they ask to change texts. They have become disengaged readers.

Other students choose books that are, in fact, at a level that is comprehensible for them. They may even believe the book will be interesting. But as they begin to read, they soon lose interest. When asked what their book is about, they cannot answer the question because their minds have been elsewhere while their eyes tracked the words. What might at first appear to be a comprehension problem is actually an issue of engagement.

Some engagement problems are temporary—students are worried about situations at home, they have problems with friends, or they don't feel well that day. But some are continual and the more time students spend disengaged from the texts in front of them, the farther they move from becoming dedicated and proficient readers. It is only through deskside conferences that I can hope to discover what stands in each individual reader's way—incomprehensible texts or uninteresting ones. And if I determine that the problem is a lack of engagement, I take deliberate steps to cure it.

Dealing with "Boring" Texts: The Abandonment Conference

By the intermediate and middle school grades, many student readers' underlying problem is that they are totally disengaged from texts. Students who can understand the books they've chosen but are bored by them concern me just as much as the students who are not understanding what they read. I truly want students to love the books they read, and early in the year I focus as much time on engagement during deskside conferences as on comprehension.

When I am sure the issue is engagement and not comprehension, my question becomes: *Why did you choose this book?* I want to hear the student verbalize the thinking she used to choose this one text from all those available to her. Often, the choice involves little, if any, thinking at all.

Students often answer this question by saying, "I don't know. I just picked it." This is the voice of a student who does not yet believe that there is *any* book in the library—or in the world, for that matter—that will be interesting. The focus of the conference then becomes the privilege of being in a reading community in which readers are given time every day to lose themselves in books they have chosen themselves. With this great opportunity comes a degree of responsibility and students must expect to find books they will finish and enjoy.

Whatever their reasons for selection, students will not grow as readers if they do not enjoy what they are reading. When developing readers spend time with books that bore them, they learn one thing: reading is boring.

When I deal with students for whom the issue is clearly engagement, I remind them that I want them to read a book they love. Then, I watch their body language. If they lean forward, ready to hear my next piece of advice, I know that they want to be engaged with texts but still have not learned how to choose them well. Many of my students, however, lean back away from me at this point in the conference. They often cross their arms over their chests, and almost always quit making eye contact with me. Their attitude is clearly, "Yeah, right. If this woman thinks there's any book in the world that I will like, she has another thing coming!"

My attitude at this point is critical. Every action taken, every word spoken in a deskside conference with a disengaged student must convey the *teacher's* belief that there is an engaging book out there somewhere in the universe that this student just hasn't found yet. But first, disengaged students must realize the reason they don't like the books they've chosen is because they didn't put enough effort into choosing them in the first place.

If students are to become lifelong readers, they must learn what genres and authors engage them. They must approach reading time as an adventure, not as a chore. But even skilled, competent, dedicated readers sometimes make bad choices. I don't finish every book I start because I don't want to spend time bored or confused when I have chosen poorly. While the main message I send is to finish books, I allow students the privilege of abandoning books they are not enjoying, but not until they can specifically tell me what they don't like about the book. "It's boring" is a general answer—and I won't accept it. My next question at that point is, "And what makes it boring?"

Sometimes this leads to a wondrous exploration of synonyms for *boring*. The book is labeled as *stupid, not interesting, dumb*. But these words are judgments—a fact I point out to the students—and judgments are opinions that must be supported with facts.

I want students to tell me *exactly* why they don't like the books they've chosen, an ability I modeled when I shared my own reading with them and showed them books I myself had abandoned. (See Chapter 2.) Sometimes students cannot connect to the characters or their situations. Sometimes the author's style is just not to their liking. Sometimes they've chosen a genre that doesn't interest them in the least. But I want the *students* to realize this is the problem. They can't make better choices until they understand the mistakes they've made choosing books.

Questions I use to help students name the reasons for not liking books might be:

- What did you expect from this book when you chose it?

- How is the book different from what you expected?

- Is there anything about the characters that keeps you from wanting to read on?

- Is there something about the way the author wrote the book that keeps you from wanting to read on?

- Is there something about the way the book is written that is confusing to you?

My role in these conferences is not to make students feel bad about making a selection that didn't work out. Rather, it is to help them discover their own reading preferences and to learn to use these to guide their book choices in the future. I want them to understand why they don't like to read because it will help them think more carefully as to what might truly engage them as readers.

I want students to take seriously the responsibility of choosing books wisely. If they can explicitly identify the mistakes they made in choosing the book they have, I make a deal with them. I will allow them to abandon the book they currently have, but they *must* finish the next book they choose. After all, allowing students to abandon book after book does not teach them to choose books that will interest them—it teaches them they can continue to hate reading.

Understanding What Keeps Readers Reading

When I start to realize that several students are going to need to choose new books, I often do a minilesson aimed at helping students understand what bogs readers down and what pushes them forward. I begin the lesson by saying, "I've noticed that several of you are having trouble staying interested in the books you've chosen. This happens to all of us as readers. Let's take just a minute and think about what things make us want to keep reading a book and what things make us want to stop." Then, I allow students to brainstorm answers to this question. During this time, I carefully guide them to be very specific and clear in their answers. Every reader in the room—no matter how skilled—has chosen poorly at some point in time. Everyone will have something to share. I always listen to students, both during minilessons and in individual conferences to better understand what makes readers want to abandon the texts they have chosen. This knowledge helps me support the developing readers with whom I work. Over the years, I have seen that there are predictable categories for poor choices. (See Figure 6–1.)

What makes readers want to keep reading?

- The book meets the reader's expectations for it.
- The reader asks questions that drive the reading forward to find the answers.
- The reader makes predictions and keeps reading to see if they are correct.
- The reader makes connections to the characters and/or situations presented.
- The reader makes connections to the topic of the informational text.
- The reader is intrigued by new information the author has provided.
- The reader is putting together the author's clues to make inferences that reading on must confirm or reshape.
- The reader is caught up in the events the author has presented.
- The book is suspenseful and the reader wants to read on to see what happens next.

What makes readers want to stop reading?

- There are too many unfamiliar words with which the reader must struggle.
- The text plays with time or has multiple plotlines that the reader is not yet sophisticated enough to handle.
- The reader doesn't know what to expect from the genre.
- The text is too easy and therefore considered childish or boring.
- The reader is word reading only and not reading for meaning.
- The reader is not generating questions to drive the reading forward.
- The reader is not formulating any predictions to drive the reading forward.
- The reader cannot or is not making connections to the content of the text.
- The reader is not making mental images to aid comprehension.
- The text is too character-driven and the reader prefers plot-driven texts.
- The reader is confused and does not use this confusion to generate questions but instead decides the book is not a good choice for him or her.
- The reader is being forced to read.
- The book is set in the past and the reader does not know how to connect to the characters and situations.
- The beginning of the book is too slow and does not hook the reader.
- The paragraphs—or the book itself—are too long.
- The reader does not understand where the author is going with the text.

Figure 6–1   *Anchor Chart for Engagement*

Dealing with Distractions

I was working with a class whose disengagement was a source of great concern to its teacher. I first observed the students for a few days—watching them in the library as they flocked to bookshelves to pretend to choose books for the day at the beginning of reading time, and watching them "pretend read" with great regularity.

My first step was to create some excitement around texts, so I took stacks of books into the room each day, fiction on some days and nonfiction on others, offering quick book talks and then stacking these books on the desk. As I walked through the room conducting conferences, students would ask to see a title that had sparked their interest, and I would go to the desk and bring them the book. Finally, I had just about everyone in a book they seemed to genuinely want to read, but the actual reading was still not going as well as I had hoped.

I noticed these students were very easily distracted. At first, I assumed they still were not engaged, which was certainly part of the problem. But as I watched the pattern of distractions more carefully, I began to notice that even the best readers in the room were distracted several times during the period.

The school had classrooms built in blocks of four. There were walls between the rooms, but no doors—just large open doorways in the corner where the four classrooms met. It was easy to hear what was happening in every nearby class. The principal also required that the one door in the room, the one that led to the outside hall, be kept open. This meant that students could easily see and hear anyone walking through the hallway. In addition, I was conferring with students in the room during the reading time. It was suddenly clear why so many students were distracted.

I started to think about my own reading. I often read in our den. The television set is usually on, and my husband is there as well. Sometimes something on TV will catch my attention; sometimes my husband will say something to me. The phone will ring. My neighbor's motorcycle will fire up. My leg will fall asleep. A detail in the text will remind me of something and my mind will wander. All readers have to learn to deal with distractions.

I had never had this discussion with students. I wondered if the most challenged readers in the room believed that when they were distracted it was because they were poor readers. I also wondered if they had any idea how to get back to the text when distractions occur.

The next day I started the class by posting an anchor chart labeled *Distractions*. Below the heading was a T-chart with no headings posted yet. I looked at the students and asked, "Do you ever get distracted when you read?" Gabriella, easily the most voracious reader in the room, joined the other students in nodding their heads and saying the equivalent of, "Sure we do."

Kendall, who sat next to Gabriella, looked at her in disbelief. "*You* get distracted?" he said incredulously. It had never occurred to him that such an accomplished reader might be dealing with distractions just like he was.

Together the students and I began to construct an anchor chart. We started on the left side of the T-chart and put up a heading that said *When I get distracted by* . . . The list was long—teachers' voices, other kids in the room, announcements over the PA, noise in the hall, what happened last night at home, just to name a few. Students were astonished to see the class's strongest readers offering many reasons for distractions.

"Readers get distracted," I began, "not because they are poor readers but because they are human. Our brains are constantly aware of our surroundings and will attend to something new in the environment to decide whether or not it is a threat to us. We need to expect distractions."

I next made the point that while distractions are to be expected, we need to acknowledge them and get back to the reading, not stay distracted. I wrote a heading on the second column: *I* . . . and asked students to offer ideas on how to get back into the text once they've been distracted. Together we went down the list, offering suggestions for how to redirect attention after a distraction. They offered ideas such as:

- When I am distracted by the nearby teacher's voice, I tell myself to ignore it and go back to the last place I remember what was going on to start reading again.

- When I am distracted by another student, I give that person a dirty look and try to find the place where I finished reading.

- When I get distracted by a long teacher announcement to the class, I try to remember what was going on when I stopped reading and go on from there. If I can't remember, I go back to the beginning of the page or chapter and start again.

For the next several days, I asked students to keep a log of their distractions. Each time something took them away from the text, they were to look up quickly and jot down the time, then get back to reading. At the end of reading time, they were to list the things that distracted them and what strategies they used to return to the text.

Interestingly, the students who logged in the most distractions were the most engaged readers in the room. The disengaged readers, on the other hand, logged in almost no distractions at all. For them, it seemed that reading itself was a distraction, demanding they leave a world where they felt comfortable and in control and enter one that provided tremendous challenges they felt poorly equipped to overcome. They didn't even seem to be aware that they were, in fact, distracted. For them, engagement was a continual challenge, one that would have to be addressed in individual deskside conferences.

By explicitly discussing distractions, students learn to expect them and plan ways to get past them and back into the text. They learn that distractions are part of a reading life, not an indicator of reading inferiority.

◎ *Handling the Distraction of Deskside Conferences*

Ann Marie Lacefield is a sixth-grade reading teacher at Spring Woods Middle School in Spring Branch, Texas, who has elevated supported independent reading to an art form. She is very generous and often lets teachers visit her classroom to see the model in action.

I was in her room with a group of teachers one day as she moved from her minilesson to her conferences. "You need to eavesdrop on a conference," I urged them. "You need to hear the way she supports their reading."

Ann Marie allows students to sit anywhere in the room to read, and most choose the floor. She quietly moves up next to them when it is their turn to confer. The observing teachers tried to stay seated at the desks they had chosen, but they couldn't hear a word Ann Marie or the student said. Eventually, they realized they would have to move to the floor next to her if they were going to listen.

I am not that quiet, though I do try to be; I watch Ann Marie in amazement every time I visit her room. Since I may never master the art of the whisper conference, I need to teach my students what to do when I am conferring with students near them. I teach them to acknowledge the distraction of my conference and get back to their reading or make a decision to join us. There's more than enough room for their thinking.

A few months ago I was working with a teacher who was just starting to implement supported independent reading in her classroom. She had asked me to come to what she considered her lowest class. The desks in her classroom are arranged in groups of four, so students are close to the person across from and next to them.

When I first begin working with a class, I always ask the teacher to identify the strongest and weakest readers in the room. I start my conferences with the strongest readers so students who already consider themselves poor readers don't feel they have a target on their backs. After a few conferences with stronger readers, I knelt down next to Chris.

Since all the students were starting new books, my minilesson had been about what to expect at the beginning of a book. As I always do when all the books are new, I was starting the conferences with the same two questions: What book are you reading? Why did you choose it?

Chris was reading *Horse Power*, a book from the Orca Current series, written for below-level middle school readers. He told me he had chosen it because it looked interesting and he liked horses. Since the book is about a girl whose mother camps out on a school playground to protest the closing of the school, I was fairly certain he hadn't previewed this book.

"Did you preview this book before you chose it?" I asked.

"Uh-huh," he answered.

"So what do you know it's going to be about?"

"It's about horses," he answered.

Just as I was about to turn to the back of the book to have Chris read the summary, I noticed that Antonio, who sat across from Chris, was looking at us and paying attention to our conversation. "Antonio," I said, "we're about to read the summary for this book. Would you like to join us?"

"Okay," he said, clearly confused. After all, shouldn't I be telling him to mind his own business and get back to work?

"Chris," I continued, "show me where to find the summary." When he turned the book to the back, I knew he at least understood that much.

"Could you read it for us, please?" I asked. Chris dutifully complied—and read it well.

"So, what do you two think this book is going to be about?" Antonio jumped in with his ideas, and Chris concurred. With a new understanding of what the story would be about, I asked Chris to read the first few pages to himself while I conferred with Antonio.

Antonio was doing quite well in the book he had chosen, so the conference was a short one. Then I returned to Chris.

"Can you tell me what's going on so far in your book?" I asked.

"I'm not really sure," Chris admitted. "It's a little confusing right here at the beginning."

I looked at the first page and realized that the book is written in first person, a point of view that often confuses unsophisticated readers. In addition, the reader has to approach this text ready to make the inferences about the main character and her family situation that will prove important later in the story.

The book begins at an airport with a girl arriving from a trip to visit her father, who lives an airplane trip away. "Who is telling this story?" I asked. "Is it the author or a character?"

"I'm not sure what you mean," Chris said.

Once again, I noticed Antonio's eyes on us—and once again I invited him in. "Antonio," I said, "would you mind helping us figure this out?"

Together the three of us looked at the beginning of the book. Although Antonio could easily understand books told from a first-person point of view, he had never spent time thinking about the difference between first- and third-person narratives. The conference would be new learning for Chris, but it would help Antonio label a literary element he already understood and validate the thinking he does to make sense of narratives.

"Look at this first part," I said. "Do you see how it uses the word *I*?"

"Yeah," Antonio jumped in. "That means it's a character talking."

"Chris," I said, "can you tell me what Antonio means by that?" By asking this question, I was validating my belief that Chris is easily as smart as Antonio, a belief that at this point Chris might not actually share.

"Well, if it says *I*, that means that somebody who's in the story is telling the story, right?"

"Yes, sir," I smiled. "And now let's see if we can figure out who that person is."

By this time, Antonio had lost interest in what we were doing and was back to reading his book. A less skilled reader might not have been able to redirect his attention so quickly, in which case I would have continued to include him in the conference so that both students would get the benefit of seeing how readers figure out who the main character is when the author has chosen a first-person point of view. This instruction is anchored in an authentic text and is given at the point of need. The eavesdropping student might not be confronting this problem today, but when he does encounter this type of writing, he will know what to do because he has been a partner in a conference that addressed this issue.

In all the years I have conducted deskside conferences with students, I have never found these conferences to impede students' learning. Do they sometimes distract students from what they are reading? I'd be lying if I didn't admit that they do. But I know from years of experience that the students who are distracted are either engaged enough readers to get back to what they were doing quickly or they are readers who can benefit from the direction the conference is taking if I invite them in. I'd rather see them distracted for a few minutes than lost or bored for thirty.

Assessing the Comprehension of Disengaged Students

I always assume first that any disengaged student's problem is comprehension, since I know that students may get lost in a book they don't understand—but it is not the version of *lost* for which I am hoping. My first questions to these readers are genre-related. I want to be certain students are aware of what they should expect from a particular genre and how this will shape their understanding of the books they hold in their hands. **The questions I usually ask first are:**

- Do you know what kind of book this is?

- Have you read other books in this genre?

- What do you expect the characters and events to be like in this kind of book?

If the student cannot answer these questions, it is time for one-on-one instruction.

I approach these deskside lessons in the same way I approach a whole-class minilesson. I have an objective in mind—to show this student how understanding what to look for at the beginning of a book improves comprehension of the text. My job is not to remind the student that I did, in fact, cover this in some detail in the lesson I gave before the book shopping spree. It is not to point out that he has this information in the reading notebook sitting on the corner of his desk. My job is to help him see that owning this knowledge will change him as a reader.

My goal in deskside conferences is to truly help student readers, so my tone of voice must convey that intent. I don't want anything about my demeanor to put the student on the defensive. I want my attitude and actions to draw students toward what I am saying, to convince them that I am giving them help, not criticism. Many of these students have already had enough criticism to last a lifetime.

If students can answer the genre questions, I know that they have at least some knowledge of what to expect from the text—but I need to probe further to see if they are actually finding these things. **My next question, then, would be:**

- Can you tell me something about the main character in this book? (for fiction)

- Can you tell me something new you've learned so far? (for nonfiction)

A student's inability to answer these questions helps me know that her understanding of genre is surface-level only and is not being used to shape her comprehension of the text. Then, I aim to support her comprehension.

To a fiction reader I might say, "Remember how you told me that this book is realistic fiction? In a fiction book, the author always provides information about the characters, setting, and problem at the beginning of the book. As readers, it is our job to look for these things. Let's go back through the pages you've read and see if we can locate some details about the main character."

To a nonfiction reader, I might say, "Remember how you told me this book is a biography? In a biography, the author always tries to provide information about someone that will help us understand how the events in his life led him to be famous enough to have a book written about him. The author is trying to give us information about this person that we may not have known before. Let's go back through the pages you've read so far and see if we can find any new information that we didn't know."

In both cases, I remind students that they need to pay attention to details—but the details in a fiction book are very different from those in a nonfiction one. I must match the guidance I give to the text the student has chosen. (See Chapters 8 and 9 for more ideas on fiction and nonfiction comprehension.)

I always direct students to go back through the pages they have already read. As they begin flipping through the pages with me, I find a good place to stop them and say, "Why don't you read this part right here to me, and stop when you hear some new information." This is my way of assessing if the book is too difficult for the reader. If students are in the first ten to fifteen pages of the book when the conference begins, I usually ask them to go back to the first page and start reading from there. If they are farther along in the book, I ask them to go back to the beginning of the chapter.

If students struggle with too many words as they read aloud, the one-on-one instruction needs to change direction. These readers need to hear that no one can easily understand a book that has too many unfamiliar words in it. I always talk about books I've tried to read in which I encountered this same problem, usually sharing the story of my first voyage through Vygotsky's *Thought and Language*. Pointing out my own struggles as a reader puts the student and me on equal footing.

Next, I always ask students if they used the five-finger rule (see Chapter 3) to choose this book—and almost always the answer is no. The focus of the conference then shifts to a review of why this step is so important. But just reviewing is not enough—I must be sure that the student understands it. I point out specific words with which the student has struggled while reading aloud to me and remind her that if she has to spend all her energy trying to figure out the words she will have very little left to read for meaning. I stress one more time that reading is not saying the words—it's understanding what the author means by them. I am going to want her to abandon this book—but not until she tells me how her thinking needs to change when she selects the next book she will read. I need to hear her identify the mistake she made in book selection and how she will avoid the same mistake in the future. Once it is clear to me that she understands the importance of reading a book that's at a manageable level of difficulty, I set her free to find another book from the classroom library that will be a better match for her stage of reading development—and once that book is chosen we will go through this series of questions and actions again until I am sure she has chosen more wisely.

◎ *Reshaping Students' Vision of Reading*

If students are not struggling with the words on the page, but are unable to tell me specifics about what they've read so far, I know that the focus of the conference will need to be on reshaping their vision of reading. Reading is not just saying the words; the words are there to convey ideas from one person, the writer, to another, the reader. Both must take part in what Rosenblatt (1965, 1978, 2005) calls a transaction. Students who are word callers, focused only on pronouncing words without considering their meaning, will not become readers until they learn to engage in this important transaction.

In these cases, the deskside teaching involves both modeling and guided practice focused on moving past pronunciation of words to understanding their meaning in the context of the book itself. I remind the students that they are to stop and comment when they find new information about a character, the setting, or the problem in fiction or about the topic of a nonfiction book. I usually laugh and say, "I think you forgot about that part!" and have them read to me again. After they have read over several new pieces of information without comment, I stop them and say, "What did you just learn about [the character, the setting, the problem, the topic]?"

Sometimes this question draws a blank expression, a stare that presents a tremendous teaching opportunity for me. When I offer focused support at students' point of need, they learn to conquer their reading challenges—to make meaning from words rather than just pronouncing them.

Next, I tell these students that as readers we need to engage with writers, following their trains of thought and letting their thinking reshape our own. I then go back to where the student began the reading and say, "I'll read to you this time—and I'll stop when something catches my attention. I am expecting to collect new information, and when I do, I will stop and think just a second about it before moving on. Sometimes the new information will change what I have been thinking up to that point."

Then I begin to read, and when I read across a new detail I stop and say, "The writer just told me . . ." If it is appropriate, I add, "I think that means . . ." showing how I use the detail to make inferences or predictions. I do this several times before asking the student to pick up where I left off and do the same thing. Before I leave the student's desk, I always ask, "So tell me what you will do today as a reader." I expect to hear a rephrasing of the lesson I have just taught in the conference. If not, I redirect one more time, again being careful of my tone of voice and making sure that any frustration I might feel is kept in check. Even if I feel that a student is not putting forth the effort I expect, I must believe that he will, and I make sure that my actions and attitudes support that expectation. When I am certain he understands what to do, I tell him that I want him to continue to collect new information, and mark these places with sticky notes so he can jot them down at the end of reading time. I check these notes to be sure he understands what to do.

Using Questions to Engage Readers

Between the Presidential election and the football playoffs last fall, I heard the word *momentum* countless times. *Webster's New World College Dictionary, Fourth Edition* (Agnes 2002) defines momentum as "strength or force that keeps growing." As political campaigns and football games continually remind us, momentum can shift at a moment's notice.

Lessons aimed at engagement followed by effective initial conferences can lull teachers into false senses of accomplishment. After a few abandoned books and various redirections, the students seem to have settled into the books they have chosen. But the work in an independent reading classroom never ends. Students who are unaccustomed to finishing books and held responsible for comprehending them will begin to stall out. Their frustrations will return unless the teacher is proactive and teaches ahead of student need. As Louise Rosenblatt (1965) advised, "The teacher's task is to foster fruitful interactions—or, more precisely, transactions—between individual readers and individual literary texts" (26). In order to "foster fruitful interactions," teachers must understand that to make sense of texts, readers must take deliberate steps to actively engage with them. Merely passing their eyes across the words will never be enough. And what students will need most—for both engaging with and comprehending the texts they have chosen—is to generate effective questions.

I have come to believe that questioning is the single most important strategy for keeping readers engaged with texts. As a skilled reader, I enter a text with questions:

Who is the main character and what is that person like? What is the problem? Or what does this character want or need? What's getting in the way of the character getting it? How do I think it will be solved? As I enter the world created for me by an author, I expect to be puzzled, to generate spontaneous questions that will force me to read ahead to find the answers. But Keene and Zimmermann (2007) remind us, "children who struggle to read don't consistently ask questions as they read—not before, during, or after. . . . They're passive as they read. They read—or they submit to the text—never questioning its content, style, or intent" (106).

Students who view themselves as poor readers believe that when they are puzzled or confused it is because they are inept readers. Instead of reading ahead to clear up these confusions, they give up and want another text, one that won't make them feel like a failure one more time. They don't know that questions drive reading forward for devoted readers.

I distinctly remember reading the first chapter of Blue Balliett's *Chasing Vermeer*. In this chapter, an assortment of unnamed people all receive cryptic letters from an unnamed source. At the end of the chapter, I still didn't know who these people were or what the purpose of the letters might be. As a proficient reader, I knew I should expect confusion at the beginning of books. I also knew I should use the questions this confusion raises to drive my reading forward. Spontaneously, the questions began—Who are these people? What do they have in common? Why were they chosen to receive these letters? Who sent them? These were questions that would not be answered until the end of the book—and as a skilled reader I was not frustrated by this. I trusted my reading abilities enough to know if I just kept moving through the text and actively looked for them, the answers would come, one new piece of information at a time. But many readers do not have this much faith in their abilities and they are unwilling to accept the confusion that texts bring. Changing attitude toward questioning can change readers.

◎ The Art of Questioning

I read the book reviews in the Sunday paper every week to help me find good new books I would enjoy reading. My family knows this, so on Christmas last year I found Tom Brokaw's *Boom! Voices of the Sixties* and Maggie O'Farrell's *The Vanishing Act of Esme Lennox* under the tree for me, gifts from my younger daughter who had heard me talk about them one Sunday.

I wanted to read these two books because the reviews sparked my curiosity.

- What new insights would I gain from Tom Brokaw's reflections on the Sixties, an era I remember very well?

- Would I see the events of this turbulent time in a different light after reading his interviews and commentary?

- How would the conclusions I drew from my own experiences during this time be reinforced or reshaped by what Brokaw had written?

- Why was Esme Lennox locked in a mental hospital for sixty-one years?

- Why did no one in the family ever discuss her?

- How will her release into her great-niece's custody affect both their lives?

I generated all these questions without reading one word of either book. I generated them from reading the publisher's summary on the dust jackets—and from knowing what to expect from the genre these two texts represent.

Developing readers seldom realize the summaries are there to prompt questions, to make potential readers so curious they just have to read the book to find the answers. Even though I teach students to read summaries and use them to determine whether or not they are interested in a book, many of them *do not* spontaneously develop questions they think the book will answer. They are missing the piece that, more than any other, keeps those of us who love reading turning the pages.

Students must be *taught* to generate effective questions. Those who are already avid readers use questions almost subconsciously as the basis of their movement through a text. Raising it to a conscious level gives them an opportunity to share their thinking with the less skilled readers in the room. But those who still see reading as something you do only in reading class will need clear explanations of the impact of questioning on their reading engagement.

Last year, I taught for a week in a sixth-grade classroom that was between teachers. Their original teacher had retired at the end of the semester, and their new teacher had to finish up paperwork and her current job before she could begin the second semester. Since the original teacher had been greatly distracted by family health concerns, the students had not received the same quality of instruction I had known this teacher to provide in previous years. The students were woefully behind in many areas, and few of them had read anything substantial all year. My goal for the week was to increase the level of engagement and to assist them in selecting appropriate books so that the independent reading part of the instructional program would start well for their new teacher.

Many of the students in this class swore they didn't like reading because, of course, "it's boring." These are the voices of developing readers who do not yet understand that reading *isn't* boring to those of us who read to find answers to our questions.

My first strategy lesson, then, was on questioning. I like to use Kate DiCamillo's *The Tiger Rising* as the anchor text for this series of lessons because the chapters are short and the questions are immediate. The book is also loaded with symbols—and eventually I want to help students see how recurring objects (in this case a suitcase and a tiger) often have deeper meanings

The first day, I showed the students the book I had chosen and read the summary on the dust jacket aloud to them. We had already created an anchor chart with the heading, *Readers,* to which we had added the key point, *choose books they expect to finish and enjoy.* Now I added a second key point: *ask questions that make them keep reading to find the answers.*

"Readers have questions before they ever open the book," I told them. "From reading the summary, I already want to know:

- Why is there a tiger in a cage in the Florida woods?

- Why do the two characters want to keep their memories locked up?

I am going to write these questions on this sheet of paper—and I am going to go into the text expecting to find the answers. I know I may not find the answers right away—really good questions force me to collect a lot of information in order to get an answer. But these two questions will guide me as I start to read."

The students had already previewed books and decided on one they thought was right for them. I asked them to reread the summaries of their books, this time thinking of at least two questions they thought the book would answer. Some students did quite well, asking questions like:

- Why did someone build the bomb that killed the little boy? (from Caroline B. Cooney's *The Terrorist*)

- What will Janie say to her parents after she sees her picture on the milk carton? (from Caroline B. Cooney's *The Face on the Milk Carton*)

- What has happened to the girl's parents? (from Joseph Bruchac's *Skeleton Man*)

These are the questions of readers who already understand that one of the key questions readers must ask in a fiction text is how the problem will be solved.

Many students, however, asked questions such as these:

- Where do they live? (from Betty Ren Wright's *A Ghost in the House*)
- Is Andy okay? (from Sharon Draper's *Tears of a Tiger*)
- Where does Darcy's mom work? (from Anne Schraff's *Someone to Love Me*)

These are the questions of readers who don't love reading. They are echoes of questions teachers have asked in the past, questions meant to make them prove they had actually read the text, though these questions did not require them to think about what they had read. Their school experiences have taught these readers that the teacher is the one who asks the questions—and their job is then to collect the details that provide the simplistic answers. When readers focus all their attention on details rather than on understanding such things as characters, their motivations, and the effect of events on their lives, they miss the point of reading.

Questioning the Author's Intent

One of the most important things I want developing readers to understand is that the texts they hold in their hands were written by actual human beings who chose every word, every character, every new bit of information for a specific purpose. This same author then put considerable effort into choosing a title that somehow ties in with the central idea of the text. When we pick up texts, we have to let the words that were chosen give us insight into the writer's mind, continually asking, "Why is this here?" Even things that seem trivial are there for a reason.

Developing readers seldom take time to question *why* something appears on the page. I remember conferring with an eighth-grade boy who was reading S. E. Hinton's *The Outsiders* with something about ten football fields short of enthusiasm. He was in one of the early chapters and had already been introduced to most of the main characters. He could name the characters and describe them, but he was not thinking about why each of them would be essential to the story that was about to unfold. The three Curtis brothers and Johnny are shown to have virtues and strengths that stand in stark contrast to the character of Dally Winston, a character drawn as the perfect picture of what was then called a juvenile delinquent. He thumbs his nose at authority and has recently been released from jail. He is the exact opposite of Darry Curtis, the responsible oldest of three brothers who finds himself the head of a household after his parents die.

After asking the student to tell me about the main characters and hearing an accurate description of each, my next question caught this young man totally off guard: "Why would S. E. Hinton have put a character like Dally in this book?"

These are the kinds of questions readers must learn to ask. They keep the reader actively involved with the author sitting on the other side of the book. I know to ask these questions because I understand that nothing in a published book is there merely to take up space—and I want students to know that, too. Every word, sentence, and paragraph has a purpose.

Questions as a Response to Engage Readers

Any response a student is asked to make to a text should be designed to offer the teacher a way to quickly assess how the student is progressing as a reader. Questioning is one of several strategies used by proficient readers (Keene and Zimmermann 2007), so asking students to generate questions in response to their reading can help me determine if they are engaged with and comprehending the texts they have chosen. But asking students to focus on *answering* these questions requires them to use some additional proficient reader strategies.

Deciding what questions to write requires students to focus on what is important in the text, another key strategy. The students who ask questions like "Where does Darcy's mother work?" are readers who get mired in the details and miss the bigger picture. A quick glance at their questions will make this clear to a teacher before a conference begins and can steer the conference towards a discussion of what things are important in the text. I ask students to guess what the answers to their questions might be, write them down, and put a question mark after them to show that this is their guess, not a definite answer. These guesses are really a form of inference, another key strategy that proficient readers use. **Students generally have one of three problems with inferring:**

- They never make inferences at all.

- They make random guesses that are not tied to the text in any way, relying instead only on their own prior experiences or expectations.

- They restate something they read in the text rather than realizing that an inference is an idea that is not written on the page.

If a student makes *no* guesses, the teacher knows that the student is not trying to read between and beyond the lines on the page. If the guesses are not tied in any way to the text but are merely random guesses based only on prior knowledge, the student does not understand reading is the process of combining what you already know from prior experiences with people, texts, and the world with specific information provided by the author of this particular text. However, if they never make guesses but merely wait to see if they can copy the answer from the text, they are dependent only on the text's words and not trusting their own prior knowledge to help them think ahead of the words.

These issues can be addressed either in minilessons or in deskside conferences, depending on how widespread the problem is. Either way, confusions discovered during a deskside conference should be clarified in that conference and not saved for a later time.

I teach students to not only make educated guesses based on the information they have collected so far in the text, but to also understand they may have to adjust their expectations based on new information the author provides. I model this with the questions and guesses I have generated with their help as we work our way through *The Tiger Rising*. This addresses the concept of synthesis, an understanding proficient readers have that their views and ideas will need to be adjusted as they read farther into a text and combine the new information provided with what they already know.

Asking students to generate questions and to answer them with both educated guesses and information given in the text is a high-yield response that teaches students:

- to use questions to drive their reading forward

- to combine the information in the text with what they already know to develop educated guesses called inferences

- to be flexible in their thinking so they are able to adjust their ideas based on new information.

Even more important, teaching students to ask effective questions will deepen both their engagement with and comprehension of the texts they read.

A Conference Focused on Questioning

Elena is a sixth grader who had chosen the book *A Ghost in the House* by Betty Ren Wright. This is her first year out of a bilingual classroom where, she admits, she rarely read books written in English, so it is very hard for her to engage with them.

Elena is a hard worker, but I was not completely sure the book she had chosen was at the proper level for her. I wanted to confer with her right away to be sure she had chosen a book she was capable of reading and understanding. I knew if the decoding load wasn't overwhelming, she would need help generating questions that would aid her comprehension.

Betty Ren Wright's books are often full of ghostly occurrences with just the right level of thrill for developing readers. But Wright believes the power of a suspense book lies in caring about the characters, so she almost always takes many pages at the beginning of the book to build a clear picture of the characters and their surroundings, settings that always impact the events significantly.

A Ghost in the House spends the first three pages talking about a girl changing a picture in the bedroom of the old house where her family is living. She wants to take down the portrait of a girl that hangs over the fireplace and replace it with a landscape she found in a storeroom. Experienced readers understand that if the author spends three pages talking about pictures at the very beginning of the book, then the pictures are going to play a key part in the story—but Elena saw it as wasted time. She wanted to get to the ghost.

Elena was on page three. "What's happening so far in your book?" I asked.

"They're just talking about some pictures," she answered.

"Really?" I continued. "Why do you think the author did that?"

Elena sat there—silent. She was waiting for me to give her the answer, but my job was to guide her, not to supply answers she could find on her own.

"You know, Elena," I began, "at the beginning of books authors are giving you important information you will need to believe what happens later. If an author spends several pages talking about one thing, that thing *has* to be important. Let's think about how these pictures might be important later. Would you read me the part where they start talking about the pictures?" I had not read this book before, so I had to use the words of the text to guide my questions.

Elena began reading from the third paragraph and read it accurately but with a noticeable lack of confidence. "Wow," I said, "you are really reading this book well. I think it's a good choice for you." Her face brightened. "If I had to read a Spanish book to you, I wouldn't be able to do it nearly that well. And I *certainly* wouldn't understand what I just read! Did you understand that part?"

"Yeah," she answered. "There's a picture of a girl over the fireplace, and she wants to take it down and put up a picture of a place."

"And what is this book called?"

"*A Ghost in the House*," she answered.

"So what do you expect to happen in this book?" I asked, sending her back to the basics of the suspense genre and to the title.

"There's going to be a ghost in it," she said.

"So how might these pictures be related to what is going to happen later?" I probed.

"Maybe the ghost will be the girl in the picture?" she asked hesitantly, unsure of her answer.

"That's certainly a possibility," I said. "So what would be a good question to ask about this part of the book?"

She thought a minute and then said, "Is the girl in the picture the ghost?"

I had given a minilesson on effective questions with the class that day, so I asked a question tied to the minilesson. "How many words would it take to answer that question?"

"Just one," she said.

"So the idea of your question is good—but the question itself isn't wide enough. Can you think of a wider question to ask?"

This is a hard concept for many developing readers who are more comfortable asking the easy questions than the more complex ones. But learning to ask what I call wider questions can change readers and their involvement with texts.

Together we decided a better question would be, "How is the picture of the girl important to the story?" This question requires deeper thinking and a more complex answer.

"Do you see how finding the answer to that question will make you keep reading?" I asked. "If you just wanted to know if the ghost is the girl in the picture, you could quit reading when you found out if it was. But by wondering why the picture of her is important, you have to read through the book and gather information to answer your question."

Elena wrote down the question we had developed together. I always ask students to skip two lines under questions they write. That way they have a place to write a guess when they think they've figured out the answer to the question or to write the definite answer when it is given in the text. If the answer they've written is a guess, I ask them to put a question mark after it; if it is information confirmed in the text, I ask them to put a period. I want students to understand that guessing is important because it shows that they are thinking. But guesses must be based on the information available at the moment—and new information might force an adjustment to the guess.

"Now, don't you already have a good guess about why the picture *might* be important?" I asked.

"I think the girl might be the ghost," she answered.

"What should you do with that guess?" I asked, again referring back to the day's minilesson.

"Write it under the question," she answered.

"And what punctuation do you put at the end?" I asked.

"A question mark," she said. She wrote her idea down.

Elena continued reading and discovered that the room had belonged to the girl in the picture, a piece of information that for the moment strengthened Elena's idea that the girl might be the ghost. Then she read right over these words: *She knew it was silly to be jealous of a girl in a painting, especially when that girl was now a sick old lady in a nursing home* (Wright 1991, 2).

When Elena finished the paragraph, I said, "So, do you still think the girl in the picture is a ghost?"

"Yes," she said. "She used to live in that bedroom, and I'll bet she wants the bedroom back."

Developing readers often ignore information that disproves their theory about a text. Elena had not understood that the sentence she had just read proved the ghost couldn't be the girl in the picture—because the girl in the picture, now an old woman, is still very much alive.

"Read the first sentence of that paragraph again," I prompted, "and remember that authors always weave new pieces of information into the story, information you need to understand the characters and the events."

Elena reread the sentence and looked at me confused. "Does that mean the girl in the picture isn't dead?"

"Good reading!" I complimented. "That's why I love Betty Ren Wright. She is great at leading us to think one thing and then giving us one little new piece of information that will make us change what we thought completely. That makes reading really fun—readers get to change their minds!"

"So I don't understand why the picture is important," Elena said.

"Did the author tell you about only *one* picture?" I asked.

Elena thought a minute. "There's the picture of that place," she said.

"Can you think of another question?" I asked.

"Is the picture of the place important?" she suggested.

"Think about that question just a minute—how many words to answer it?" I reminded.

"One—so I need to change it," she realized.

"Look at the question you just wrote," I said. "See if that helps you write a new one."

"How is the picture of the place important?" she wrote—the perfect choice!

"Now I think you're ready to read on," I said. "Keep looking for information about these pictures—but pay attention to other things she talks a lot about. If the author spends a lot of time giving details about something, like she did with those pictures, that something is important."

Elena continued to need help recognizing important elements in the text, but she made progress and worked her way successfully through a book that was at the top of her instructional level. With continued support, this book offered a vehicle for her growth as a reader.

Questions for Reflection

Understanding the importance of engagement changes the way we approach our students as readers. As you begin to plan instruction that addresses engagement, consider these questions:

- How many of your students are choosing books they really intend to read?

- Have you modeled the reasons why you abandon texts so your students understand they can't just label a text as boring?

- How will you handle students who continually abandon books?

- How many of your students are distracted during independent reading time—and how can your instruction help them deal with this challenge?

- Could a discussion of what keeps readers reading help your students become more engaged with texts?

- Have you used instructional time to model how questioning keeps readers engaged with texts?

- Have you taught your students that an author wrote the words they are reading and that every word is put there for a purpose?

If we make intentional efforts to address the issues that keep students from engaging with texts, we can help them take giant steps toward becoming lifelong readers.

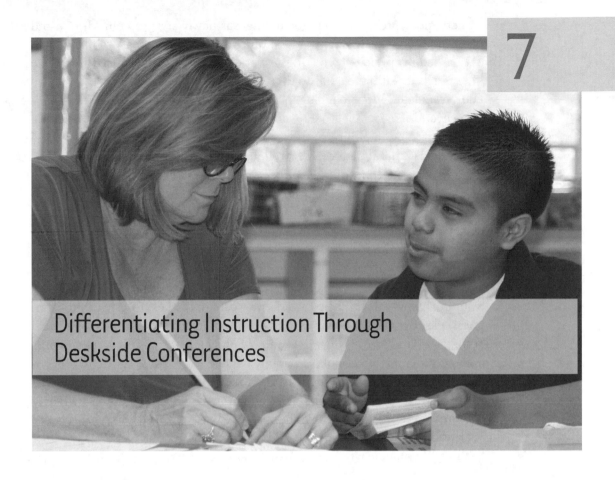

Differentiating Instruction Through Deskside Conferences

When I was a student in the classroom many years ago, the expectation was that the teacher would deliver a lesson, the students would pay attention, the teacher would then assign work, and the students would complete it. We all got the same lesson and the same assignment and no one thought a thing about it.

But the world was a much different place back then. The term *learning disabilities* had not been invented yet and students who may have had them were often "held back." Everyone in my school spoke English, so second-language learners were those of us on the "college track" who took Spanish or Latin in high school.

When I began my teaching career in El Paso, Texas, in 1971, I had no students with Individual Education Plans (IEPs) and, believe it or not, no students who didn't speak English as their primary language—at least, not until December, when Fernanda entered my classroom. She was newly arrived from Mexico and enrolled in my freshman English class. She did not speak one word of English. When I asked my principal what in the world I was supposed to do with her, he told me to let her sit there. And so that is what I did.

Four years later, I was teaching in a small school district south of Houston. I had no second-language learners—but I did have a senior named Seth with a diagnosed learning disability. Seth was a fresh-faced, freckled farm boy with a sunny smile. At that time, I was experimenting with individual reading assignments (not self-selected, of course, because *I* knew what my students should read), and Seth apparently expressed some concern to his counselor. The counselor called me in and said that Seth had something called dyslexia, a term neither I nor any of my colleagues had encountered before. I was told he had trouble reading so I should not make him do it. But, once again, I knew better—so I assigned Seth to Steinbeck's *Of Mice and Men* and dug my heels in, determined he should read it. After all, this novel was very short with few vocabulary words he wouldn't know. I thought that would take care of his pesky dyslexia problem.

For weeks, Seth dutifully sat with the book while others around him finished such things as du Maurier's *Rebecca* and Twain's *Huckleberry Finn*. As students completed their assigned books, I happily handed them the tests I had ordered from Perfection Form and graded them on their "understanding." Finally, Seth said he had finished his book and I gave him his test, which, of course, he failed. His failure had nothing to do with me, I assured myself. I was probably the first teacher who had ever really expected him to read anything.

Seth and Fernanda, wherever you are, I am truly sorry.

Today's Reality

Today, teachers are faced with significant challenges when planning their instruction. They are expected to meet the needs of every student in their class and this often includes students with special education modifications who are being placed in mainstream classes, students with Section 504 modifications that must be made, and English-language learners at various levels of competence in the language of instruction. Mixed in with all these challenges are "regular education" students at all levels of proficiency.

The task of meeting all these individual needs is daunting. How can I choose the right text for each individual reader? How can I plan lessons that account for varying levels of mastery? How can I move ahead when so many of my students are lagging behind?

I take my responsibility to meet these needs very seriously. I never want to make the same instructional mistakes I made all those years ago with Fernanda and Seth. Perhaps if I had known about supported independent reading when they walked through the door of my classroom, I would have handled things differently. I would not have let Fernanda just sit there. I would not have chosen a book for Seth and required him to read it—and I certainly wouldn't have given him a test that I hadn't even written myself. If I had known how to meet these two students where they were and help them with the problems they were facing, I would not have failed them so miserably.

But I know better now.

Differentiating Instruction for Independent Readers

A differentiated classroom enables all students to reach their full potential. The content is adjusted to meet varying needs. The teacher still must deliver the curriculum mandated by the district and the state, but the curriculum is broadened to include the needs of the individual students in the room.

Students who are still grappling with grade-level skills are given individual help. Students whose skills have surpassed what is expected by the curriculum writers are given challenges and instruction that pushes them to grow as well. And students who are learning to deal with texts written in a language different from the one spoken in their homes are steered to books with their needs in mind and they are given the support they need to read them.

In independent reading classrooms, students show their mastery of the content through varied means. Written reading responses can be adjusted to meet the needs of the individual learner; book discussion topics can be varied to allow even the most challenged of readers to participate. Individual conferences give students a chance to discuss their understandings and confusions in a safe environment that nurtures their growth. Reading responses, book discussion prompts, and conference questions are all designed to meet each learner at his or her particular point of need.

But deskside conferences are the heart of differentiation in an independent reading classroom. These individual moments set aside for readers to talk about their successes and challenges are different for every student.

No matter what other label students may bring with them, reading classrooms are basically filled with three types of readers: those who are progressing as expected, those who have fallen behind, and those who are surging ahead. The reasons they advance or fall behind is purely individual. Test scores and grades might show me who "gets it" and who doesn't, but they can never tell me why. Only my coaching conversations with students who are learning the habits of readers can unlock the mysteries of my students' achievement—or lack thereof.

Delayed Readers

I do not like the term *struggling reader*. Teachers use this phrase to describe all the students in their classrooms who are not making the progress they had hoped, but the term *struggling* is a misnomer. According to *Webster's New World College Dictionary, Fourth Edition* (Agnes 2002), to *struggle* is to "make great efforts or attempts; strive; labor." In most cases, it is not the students but their *teachers* who are laboring with great and continued effort. Many of the students quit "struggling" ages ago. Like an adventurer trapped in quicksand, they have quit fighting it; they are floating on their backs, accepting their fate, and waiting for someone to rescue them.

Webster's defines the word *delay*, however, as "to put off to a future time; postpone." If a plane flight is delayed, it will, in fact, arrive eventually and the passengers will, indeed, reach their destination. They won't get there when they were expected, but they will achieve their goal of traveling from Point A to Point B.

Below-level readers can be seen in this same light. They are not struggling; they are delayed. They have not developed reading skills and proficiencies on the planned schedule, but they are capable of catching up. They will need to be carefully assessed to determine the reasons for their delay and then provided with opportunities to strengthen the reading muscles they will need to accelerate their progress. It means they will need more focused attention than some of the other readers in the room who are sailing along at the expected speed—and they will definitely need to consume words at a rate far above what they have done in the past. But it does *not* sentence them to a lifetime of below-level reading performance.

◎ The Emotions of the Delayed Reader

Research has given us valuable insight into the workings of the human brain. One body of research with immense implications for delayed readers is the research into emotions, particularly the brain's reactions to a perceived threat. When the brain perceives a person is threatened in some way, it immediately kicks into the "fight or flight" mode, operating purely on emotion for the moment. Once the brain takes a closer look at the stimulus and determines it is not, in fact, a threat, emotions calm down and the individual is able to respond more rationally. But what if the brain determines that person *is* being threatened? What happens then?

Emotion overrides thinking when people are threatened. At this point, in fact, people revert to survival mode in what Caine and Caine (1994) call downshifting and Goldman (1995) calls an emotional hijacking. Once individuals feel threatened they can see only two choices—fighting the thing that threatens them or running from it.

This is the situation that intermediate and middle school delayed readers encounter every day. They are continually asked to perform tasks for which they are not yet fully equipped, not just in reading class but in content classes throughout their school day. They know they have never been good at reading—the neon lights of failed tests and failed subjects have flashed in their faces for as long as they can remember. And they are still children, no matter how mature their bodies may appear. They respond in a purely human manner. They either flee from reading by pretending to do it or they fight their inadequacies by continuing to try to read books they don't understand or by acting out in class. Their continued inability to engage with texts leaves them farther and farther behind the students who are actually making expected progress—and the level of the threat increases as time goes on.

Delayed Readers in the Classroom

By the intermediate grades, delayed readers fall into two broad categories: those who are still trying and those who have already given up. By middle school, almost all of these challenged readers fall into the latter category and are not even pretending they care about reading. Whether they are receptive or hostile, the teacher's job as their guide is to spend enough individual time with these readers to begin to understand what is blocking their reading progress and then to offer focused support to engage them with texts, improve their skills, and lead them to a lifelong love of reading.

I know a delayed reader when I see one. It is the girl who never has a book at her desk ready to read. It is always at home or in her last period class or lost somewhere in the great unknown. "I'm sorry, miss," she'll say. "I'll get another one."

It is the boy who doesn't get out his reading log or response journal—and dares me to notice and correct his behavior. He sits with arms crossed, head tilted back, feet splayed into the aisle. "Log in on your reading log," I remind him. Who knew it could take so long to write a page number on a piece of paper? And who knew it would require so much sighing?

It is the girl who refuses to read at all unless I personally sit with her and get her started. And she will quit the minute I walk away.

It is the smiling boy who dutifully opens his book, logs in, and attempts to read it. He hopes his expression does not betray the fact that he is not understanding a thing he is reading. But his narrowed eyes and furrowed forehead give him away.

Whatever their demeanor, these students are keenly aware of the threat posed by this task they are ill-equipped to complete. And the threat will not go away until I equip them with the skills and confidence they need to become true readers.

◎ A Conference with a Delayed Reader

Amir is a starving reader. Starving readers really want to read. They look at other students in the room who seem lost in the books they have chosen and want desperately to find that same type of pleasure in texts. But no matter how hard they try, they can't seem to make the words on the page make sense. They are hungry for guidance that will lead them to success. In a conference with a starving reader, my focus is on the basic strategies that skilled readers use to understand what they are reading.

Many of us have driven in fog and made it safely to our destinations, but much of the scenery along the way was missed, which is particularly disappointing if the view was the reason for the trip in the first place. That is how Amir reads. He spends so much time just trying to stay on the road, focusing on decoding and making it to the next sentence, picking up just enough meaning to keep him headed in the right direction. But along the way he misses so much of what the author has put there to help him enjoy his journey—and he does realize—and regret—that he is missing all that scenery. The focus of the conference for a student like Amir should be on helping him learn how to clear away the fog.

This particular day, Amir was reading a Geronimo Stilton book. This series is cleverly designed, a great mixture of texts, graphics, and color, which is pleasing to the eye. "What are you reading today?" I asked. "It looks really interesting."

Amir showed me the cover of his book, smiling. He did not tell me the title or even say that it is a Geronimo Stilton book.

"It's a good book, Mrs. Allison."

"It looks like a good book, Amir. What is it about?"

"This mouse wants to go to Egypt, but then he decides not to go."

I was fairly certain that Amir had missed something along the way. "I've never seen one of these books before, Amir," I began. "Do you mind if I look at it?"

I picked up the book and read the summary on the back, which explained that poor, overworked Geronimo kept planning vacations and then emergencies at work would make him miss his plane. This certainly was not Amir's take on the story.

Motivated readers with whom I have worked are grateful for guidance—they just are not aware that they need it. I chose my words carefully for my conference with Amir.

"Amir, you are on the right track. Geronimo *did* plan to go to Egypt—but I think you missed something important about why he didn't go. Would you mind if we go back and reread that part?"

"That'd be great, Mrs. Allison," Amir smiled, obviously relieved.

I had to decide the best focus for learning for Amir. Since his teacher had been working on plot structure with the class, I decided to see if he understood what kinds of information are given in the beginning of a book.

I pointed to the "plot mountain" poster (Figure 7–1) that his teacher had posted in the front of the room. "Remember when we drew that mountain and explained to you how authors plan stories?" I asked.

"Yeah," Amir grinned.

"Can you explain that to me, Amir?" I asked.

He sat and thought a minute, very eager to please me by knowing exactly what to say. Finally he admitted, "I'm not really sure I understand that part, Mrs. Allison."

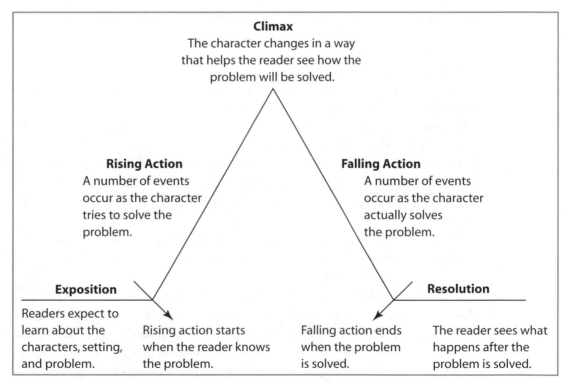

Figure 7–1 *Plot Structure/"Plot Mountain"*

So, I began to reteach, hoping to start from a point that was clear to him. "Okay, Amir," I began, "when we read a story, what are the five important parts?"

"Character, setting, events, problem, and solution," Amir rattled off. "I remember that because of that sentence *Cinderella saw every pretty star.*"

"That is great, Amir," I smiled. "Now let's think about what the author does with those five elements at the beginning of a story.

"When an author starts a story, he starts here on the flat ground," I said, drawing a plot mountain on a sheet of paper and pointing to the left side of the chart. "We come into the story not knowing anything. We don't know any characters' names or if the story will take place in Texas or at the North Pole! We don't even know what the problem will be yet. We can get some of this information from the summary on the back of the book—but that won't give us all the information we need. We need to *expect* to find out all this stuff as we begin to read—we should be *looking* for information about the character, the setting, and the problem right from the beginning."

With that information in mind, Amir and I started again from the beginning. His instructions were to stop me every single time he learned something new about the character, the setting, or the problem. The book opened with Geronimo complaining how hot it was that August—and I stopped Amir. "What did you just learn?" I asked.

"He's hot," Amir said.

"Why is it so hot?" I asked.

He was obviously stumped. "Reread that last sentence," I said, "and listen for the information about what time of year it is."

As soon as he read the word *August*, a light went on for Amir. "It's AUGUST!" he screeched. "That's why it was so hot!"

"Exactly!" I smiled. "*That* is some good reading! Do you think that maybe you missed some other things here at the beginning that might be important?"

Amir is always honest—because he always truly wants to learn. "Yeah," he said, "I think I did."

"Okay, let's think of a way to help you catch all those details you missed the first time through. Do you think an organizer would help?"

"Yeah, it might," he said

I asked if I could borrow a sheet of paper and then wrote C, S, P down the side—for characters, setting, and problem—leaving plenty of space to fill in information for each one. "These are the important things you have to figure out at the beginning of the book. Every time you learn something new about one of these things today, I want you to quickly write them down here—just enough words to help you remember. I'll check back with you at the end of reading time."

I kept my eye on Amir the rest of the time, watching him sit up straight, smile, and jot something down on his organizer as he read. When I went back at the end of the reading time, he had figured out that it was time for Geronimo's vacation—but everyone at the newspaper where he worked depended on him. As he was showering to leave for trip 1, the phone rang, he had to rush back to his office, and he missed his plane. "So, what is Geronimo's problem?" I asked.

"His work keeps calling him for help and then he misses his plane," Amir explained. Finally, he understood.

For that day, Amir had made progress. But he still would need regular conferences, and his responses needed to be assessed daily. As soon as he seemed confused again, another conference added one more piece of the reading puzzle so he could begin to understand on his own.

On-Level Readers

For too long, educators accepted the fact that some students just were not achieving and offered many logical reasons why this was true. It is no wonder that politicians have called educators to task and forced them to raise their expectations. But all the current emphasis on students who are not reaching expected levels of proficiency leaves those who are at grade level in the shadows. If all the attention is directed to those who are behind, what will happen to those who have—to this point—kept up?

Because teachers must focus more and more attention on below-level readers in order to meet the demands of current legislation, many on-level readers have been left mostly to their own devices. They are often taken for granted—just give them a book and ask them to read it and all will be well. But, all is *not* well with many of these readers; they are often some of the most disengaged readers in the room. No one has shown interest in their reading in a while because they are doing just fine—so they often take very little interest in reading themselves. Although these students are very capable of reading, their motivation often wanes. Lesesne (2006) maintains that 75 percent of graduating seniors in high school vow to never read a book again. Surely teachers want a better reading future than this for their students.

There is a real danger that on-level students will stall in their development if they, too, are not provided with focused instruction designed to help them grow. Fountas and Pinnell (2001) point out that texts at advanced levels include more complex sentences, more multisyllabic words, more sophisticated and mature themes and ideas, and more literary features such as figurative and literary language. Readers are asked to do increasingly more inferring and to track more characters and subplots. Theme, symbolism, tone, and mood assume more and more importance.

Peer culture can work against on-level students. In far too many classrooms at every socioeconomic level a pernicious attitude sets in that it's not cool to be smart or to like reading. We can't eavesdrop on every student exchange in the hallway and outside of school, but we must work even harder to redirect students' antiacademic attitudes. If teachers decide that on-level readers no longer need help, these students are in danger of being like the baseball player who is so excited about the ball he hit over the left-field fence for a walk-off homerun that he forgets to tag home plate as he goes by. Teachers have celebrated too early—and their students are the ones who will pay.

◎ The Needs of On-Level Readers

By the time they reach the intermediate grades, on-level readers have mastered the skill of decoding. They will, like all readers, sometimes encounter words that are unfamiliar and may have trouble pronouncing them, but at least they will be able to make a credible attempt. They will understand how fiction texts are constructed, though they may still find nonnarrative expository texts challenging. Many of them, however, are stuck in a genre or in a series; many are only going through the motions. Their ability to perform at expected levels on assessments has given them the enviable ability to fly under the radar—and unless teachers realize their needs are worthy of focused attention, these readers are in danger of stalling out and failing to make continued progress.

Students who are proficient in grade-level texts may continue to read at this comfortable level and not make the leap to more sophisticated reading unless supported by a more skilled reader who can help them manage the challenges higher-level texts provide. Because supported independent reading gives teachers time to work with every reader in the room, teachers are better able to meet the needs of these proficient but still growing readers.

◎ Pushing On-Level Readers

Because they are reading "on level," these readers are ready to branch out and explore new genres, learning what to expect from each one along the way. They have met educational expectations because they have been reading, but many have now reached a plateau and are rapidly losing interest in the books they once loved.

These students need the benefit of teachers who understand that readers go through predictable phases on their way to a lifelong dedication to reading. Many who once enjoyed chapter books in the phase known as "unconscious delight" (Carlsen 1994) are now ready to move on to the phase where they read about people whose situations and problems arc much like their own in a phase Lesesne (2006) has termed "reading autobiographically." Later they will want to read about places and experiences they have never known and live out the adventures through characters in books or they will want to explore philosophical issues that interest them (Carlsen 1994). By understanding the progression of reading interests, we can nudge these capable readers into new genres that may captivate them and keep them on track in their development.

As I work with these readers whose scores tell me they are proficient, I need to remember their proficiency may be minimal and in jeopardy unless I continue to help them engage with texts and learn more about the various types of reading they can explore. My goal is to help them read with a sense of joy rather than with a sense of duty so they will continue to be both capable and dedicated readers.

◎ *A Conference with an On-Level Reader*

Marcus is a page turner. Page turners are students who are perfectly willing to have a book, log it in on their reading logs, hold it in front of them for thirty minutes, and regularly turn the pages. They just are not willing to actually read it. They have been playing the independent reading game a long time. But the rules must change. The focus in these conferences goes beyond looking at the words the author has put on the page to understanding the author's purpose.

Marcus is a delightful young man—perpetually upbeat, socially strong with both adults and peers, compliant, and attentive. He just doesn't particularly like to read. His mother takes him to the city library and buys him books at book stores. He is *never* without a book—or a perceived intention to read it. The actual reading, however, often does not happen.

Marcus does not change books every day—he keeps one about the amount of time he figures I would believe it takes him to read it and then he produces a new one. His responses are skeletal, but sometimes close enough that they might not draw my attention. But when I ask him what has happened in his book so far, the lack of specificity in his responses clearly shows he is either not reading or not comprehending.

This particular day Marcus was "reading" the biography of a wrestler. He had been "reading" it for a couple of days and was now on page 37. I approached his desk and said, "A wrestling book, huh? What have you learned that's interesting?"

"Well, there's this guy named Stone Cold Steve Austin, and he's a professional wrestler."

Obviously Marcus knew this before he ever picked up the book, so I pushed harder. "What can you tell me about him?"

"Well, he's a really good wrestler. A lot of people really like him."

"Is that why you chose this book?"

"Yeah, I'm interested in pro wrestling."

"This book is a biography. Biographies help us learn what well-known people are like in their real lives. What have you learned about Steve Austin as a person?"

"He's a really good wrestler."

And the cycle continues.

It could be that Marcus was just in a book he couldn't understand, but when I asked him to go back to the beginning and read the first several pages to me, it was clear that this book was a good choice for him; he just had not been reading it. His eyes may have been going across the words—but his mind had been elsewhere the whole time.

"Marcus," I began, "I feel like you haven't really been *reading* this book—you've just been holding the book and looking at the words. *Reading* in nonfiction means you're trying to learn something from the words on the page—do you feel like you've learned very much?"

"Not really, Mrs. Allison," he admitted sheepishly.

"The good news is that that isn't happening because you *can't* read this book—you just haven't been doing it. Is that a fair thing to say?"

"Yes, ma'am."

"Okay—tell me what you want to do. Do you think you can start over with this book with the intention of actually reading it or do you need to pick another?"

"I'll start this one over."

"Okay, that sounds like a good plan. I'm going to come back to you near the end of reading time and let you tell me what you've learned about Steve Austin today—okay? When we read nonfiction, we should *always* expect to learn something new."

Marcus now had a purpose for reading. There had been a clear explanation of what he should expect from biographies and he was allowed to decide whether or not he would continue in the book he had. He will still need to be checked on regularly—when book holders know their teachers are serious about them actually reading, they usually actually read.

Gifted Readers

Even though gifted students have just as many special needs as their learning-disabled classmates, the current emphasis on every child performing at grade level works against them. These students left grade level in the dust long ago. They are often given more grade-level work rather than work at a higher intellectual level—and they are constantly asked to help their struggling classmates, who often resent the help.

This is one reason why, according to DeLisle and Galbraith, "Some of the most talented students in the United States actually choose to drop out of school altogether" (2002, 28). Reis and McCoach list "underchallenging, slow-moving classroom experiences" (2002, 83) and the need to conform to their peers as reasons why many gifted students suddenly become underachievers.

In classrooms filled with students of varying abilities and interests, it is often the gifted child who becomes invisible to the teacher. These students can perform on grade level with very little effort, and much of their teacher's time and energy is focused on the students who are *not* performing as well.

Unless we make a commitment as educators to notice the gifted children with whom we are privileged to work and offer them the same level of challenge placed in front of the other students in the room, we are accepting and even encouraging their underachievement. Rimm (in Winebrenner 2001) cautions that "when gifted children lack motivation, it is not genetic but taught" (xi).

As teachers, we have a professional responsibility that all the children with whom we work, including the gifted ones, are challenged to develop their full potential. Even gifted children should be presented with texts for which they will need teacher support and guidance. They should not be sent off to a corner of the classroom to work independently on assignments that fail to challenge or interest them.

Finding books at appropriate reading levels for gifted intermediate students presents its own set of challenges, since many of the books at the proper level deal with issues and ideas that are far above the emotional maturity of these students. These higher-level books are written for adolescents who are beginning to grapple with such things as identity and sexual encounters. Books written for this age are more graphic and contain more profanity than those written for younger students. There are, however, many books written at a lower reading level, such as Spinelli's *Maniac Magee,* that offer a great deal of complexity if the reader is prompted to look for it. These students are not too young to learn about more sophisticated devices such as symbolism, motifs, and antiheroes.

Because supported independent reading individualizes instruction, it is a powerful vehicle for working with gifted students in a regular classroom setting. Supported independent reading gives these students a chance not only to move at their own pace but also to dig more deeply into texts than they have before.

Many of the gifted students with whom I have worked trade speed reading for deep understanding. They can breeze through texts at a lightning pace, astounding their classmates with their ability to read the newest Harry Potter book in a weekend. But these students are not as challenged by reading longer texts as they could be by reading texts more carefully.

◎ *A Conference with a Gifted Reader*

Felix is a speed reader. If reading were a highway, he would have been given so many tickets by now he would never drive again. For him, reading is effortless; he has been known to start, finish, *and* comprehend up to ten books a week. He delights in taking books other students have finished and breezing through them in less than a day, *not* to the delight of his classmates. His entire reading identity seems to be tied up in reading faster and more prolifically than anyone else. But he is not seeing all the wonderful layers of meaning evident in many of the texts he is jetting through, even though he is intellectually capable of doing so.

One book he started during independent reading time and finished overnight was Louis Sachar's amazing *Holes*. This book has many layers of meaning and incredible artistic devices, including frequent flashbacks that wind up tying various story lines together. Felix had watched several classmates take two weeks or longer to read this book, but they had rejoiced in such things as discovering that Zero and Madame Z were related. Felix read right through that part as if it weren't amazing at all.

The other students were astounded he finished that book overnight but felt somewhat vindicated when, uncharacteristically, he failed a test on it. Even that didn't seem to faze Felix. When I asked him why he thought he did so poorly on the test, he just said, "Maybe I read it too fast."

I wanted him to understand exactly how much he had missed. "Felix," I said, "*Holes* is one of the best books I've ever read. It is beautifully written and carefully structured and every single detail is important. Sachar did a masterful job of creating characters we would love and dropping hints about how their pasts and their futures would intertwine. Did you catch *any* of that?"

"I like the book, Mrs. Allison," Felix said, eager to pick up the Charlie Bones book he had started that day. "I just read it too fast. No big deal."

"Felix," I said, "It *is* a big deal. You are such a good reader—but you seem to think reading a book quickly is more important than reading it well."

Felix looked at me like I had just landed from another planet. "I don't understand what you mean," he said.

"You read *Holes* in less than twenty-four hours. I'm a fast reader, too, but I slow down when I read beautifully written books so that I can think about all the incredible things the author has done. Even Stanley's name is a masterful touch—it's the same when read forward or backward. Every character's name is perfect and significant in some way. And the way he plays with time, using the past to drop hints about how Stanley's problem will eventually be solved—that book didn't just happen. It was carefully crafted by a master storyteller—and it deserved the Newbery award it won."

Felix continued to give me that creature-from-another-planet stare. "Great, Mrs. Allison, I'm glad you really liked that book. Now can I get back to Charlie Bones?"

The first chapter of *Holes* is a masterpiece full of irony and intentionally short sentences. Felix could tell me that the story took place at Camp Green Lake but was reluctant to waste any energy on the reason why Sachar would have set this story in such an odd place. Even after I explained the idea of irony, Felix continued to be interested *only* in getting me to release him from any obligation of thought so he could fly through the Charlie Bones book sitting on his desk at the moment.

Felix already has enough problems relating to the mere mortals around him, none of whom understand his desire to be a paranormal investigator when he grows up, since none of them is quite sure what that is. Felix marches to a different drummer, as do many gifted students. His only connection to the students around him is his reading of the same books they read—he does not *want* to read them differently.

Speeding readers need to be slowed down *before* they begin a text. They need to be steered to texts that will lend themselves to a higher level of thought and an examination of author's craft. (See Figure 7–2.) Then they must be given response assignments that help them master these higher-level skills.

The Rewards of Supporting Independent Readers

A requirement that teachers differentiate their instruction to meet the needs of their students provides a significant challenge for today's educators. Deskside conferences during supported independent reading provide a structure for

Holes by Louis Sachar

Walk Two Moons by Sharon Creech

The Last Book in the Universe by Rodman Philbrick

The Giver by Lois Lowry

The Westing Game by Ellen Raskin

Chasing Vermeer by Blue Balliett

Red Rider's Hood by Neal Shusterman

Criss Cross by Lynne Rae Perkins

Whirlygig by Paul Fleischmann

Things Not Seen by Andrew Clements

The Afterlife by Gary Soto

Kira-Kira by Cynthia Kadohata

Stargirl by Jerry Spinelli

Maniac Magee by Jerry Spinelli

The Outcasts of 19 Schuyler Place by E. L. Konigsberg

The Same Stuff as Stars by Katherine Paterson

Seek by Paul Fleischmann

Tangerine by Edward Bloor

The Only Alien on the Planet by Kristen D. Randle

The Tale of Desperaux by Kate DiCamillo

The Tiger Rising by Kate DiCamillo

Figure 7–2   *Books to Focus Gifted Readers on Higher-Level Thinking*

easily meeting this challenge. Students are assessed in and guided through books they have chosen and are motivated to read. Teachers meet them at their points of confusion and offer advice to help them meet the demands of increasingly complex texts. Rather than being overwhelmed by the needs of a classroom full of diverse learners, teachers are able to provide focused, individualized instruction that helps *all* students grow.

Students in this environment learn to view themselves as readers. They see themselves as competent problem solvers who can meet challenges head on and use deliberate means to overcome them. They know what kinds of books engage them and understand the craft behind an author's words. They learn to read with joy.

But an independent reading classroom that includes supported independent reading nurtures teachers as well as students. By working every day with developing readers, teachers come to a deep understanding of the nature of reading and the challenges it presents. Teachers grow as educators as much as students grow as readers. They learn to teach with confidence and joy.

Questions for Reflection

Deskside conferences help both teachers and students grow. As you think about implementing deskside conferences in your own classroom, consider these questions:

- How might you remind yourself to listen carefully to students as they share their challenges and successes with you? Have you tried counting thirty seconds as you await a student's response?

- Do you catch yourself posing a question and then rephrasing it or rushing in with an answer too soon—before the child has a chance to speak?

- What might help you strike the right balance between "stealing the hard work" from the student and not prompting enough?

- In another light, how might you become more forthright about offering advice to students and watching to see if that advice helps them become better readers?

- In general, think about ways you can become a keen observer of each of your students. What is the body language telling you? Voice? Level of eye contact? What do you know about the student's life in school and outside of school that can inform your "read" of the child? If the spirit of the conference doesn't seem convivial, why might that be so? What might you be doing to close down a student's thinking and comfort?

- Do you feel comfortable pushing even your most accomplished readers to read more widely and deeply?

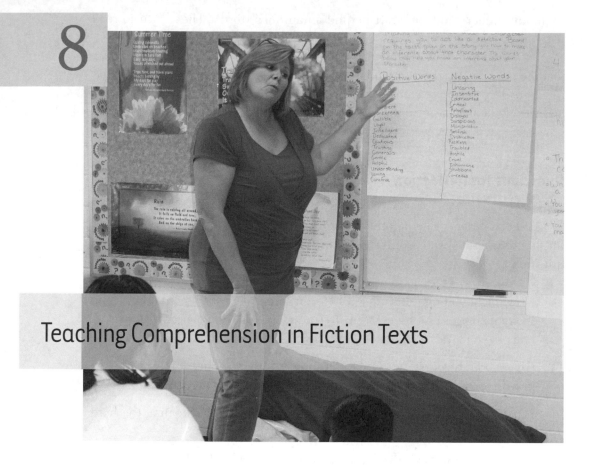

8

Teaching Comprehension in Fiction Texts

ngagement and comprehension are inseparable. They are the twin factors that contribute to our students' success as readers. Besides taking deliberate actions to keep my students engaged, I must also address any confusion they might have that keeps them from understanding a text they truly want to read.

Sometimes kids are just in over their heads. When the Harry Potter books first arrived on the scene, everyone wanted to read them. Those books are full of words that are unfamiliar to even the most skilled readers—names of characters, dormitories, potions, and spells—because J. K. Rowling made them up. On top of that, these books are long and require tremendous stamina on the part of the reader.

During this Harry Potter era, I was teaching in an intermediate school and fifth and sixth graders were a perfect target audience for Harry's exploits. But many of our students were second-language learners and delayed readers;

Junie B. Jones and Goosebumps books were much more in their range. They needed to consume many more words and increasingly longer books before they would be ready to tackle Rowling's magical world. They needed my guidance to choose books with increasingly more complex plots and my support as they learned to conquer the challenges these books would present. With this sort of daily intervention, they could develop the skills needed to follow Harry Potter to Hogwarts and feel a part of the action there—but they weren't ready yet.

If I am to successfully support my students every day, I need to be aware of the challenges that face them in the texts they have chosen, whether these books are fiction or nonfiction. Both my minilessons and my conferences must prepare my students for the challenges of increasingly sophisticated text.

Redirecting Growing Readers

I want my students to grow as readers but not to overreach. As an independent reading teacher, my first goal in deskside conferences is to determine whether students are reading books that match their interests and abilities. If they have chosen a book where issues of decoding and stamina will defeat them and move them away from a love of reading, I want to help them find a book that is a better choice.

For students who are significantly below grade level, nudging them toward the proper choice often involves dealing with their pride. If everyone else is carrying around Harry Potter, they feel childish walking around with Junie B. Jones.

Dominic was just such a student. He rushed toward me in the hallway one Monday, grinning from ear to ear. "Look what my mom bought me!" And there in his backpack was a Harry Potter book.

At that particular moment, Dominic was having trouble understanding a Herbie Jones book he had chosen in the library. He was not picking up on character clues, couldn't keep the characters straight, and was having trouble every single day remembering what happened in the book the last time he read it. How would he *ever* make it through five hundred pages of sophisticated fantasy?

I was not about to tell this child that there was no way he was going to make it through that book. The truth is he *could* read Harry Potter someday, just not yet. I decided the best tactic for him was to let him try and discover for himself that he was trying to grow too fast as a reader. It wouldn't take too many pages of Harry Potter before he and I would need to have the really important discussion, the one that reminded him that reading books that confuse us because they are above our current reading levels does not make us better readers.

Dominic was only on chapter 3 of Herbie Jones, but I let him switch to Harry Potter because he was so excited. He showed everyone in the room his new treasure. Then when supported independent reading time began, he cracked his new book open and began to read.

I watched his expression go from excitement to confusion to despair. It didn't take too many paragraphs before he realized he was drowning in a sea of words. I conferred with other readers for about fifteen minutes before I moved in next to him for the conference I had known since that morning would be inevitable today.

"How's the book going?" I asked.

"Oh, it's great!" he assured me, wanting to save face.

"What's happened so far?" I asked.

Sitting up straight in his chair and smiling, Dominic began. "Well, see, Harry is a wizard. Well, he's not a wizard yet, but he's in school to learn how to be a wizard. And he has this neat flying broom and he knows how to do spells. This is really a cool book."

Anyone who has ever read a Harry Potter book knows the book always starts in London, not at Hogwarts School. Everything Dominic had just told me came from his conversations with other people, not from his reading that day.

"Ah, so he's a wizard, is he?" I asked. "Let's read a little bit from where you are right now."

Dominic's smile faded quickly, but he knew the drill. I asked him to read to me every day, always checking to be sure he was decoding well and picking up on clues in the text. Dutifully, he began to struggle through the text.

I stopped him after about four paragraphs. "Whew—that was a lot of work for you!" I said.

"Yeah," he smiled, "there's a lot of hard words in this book."

"And this is a really long book," I said, flipping through the pages to the end. "And you haven't even finished Herbie Jones yet. Do you think it would be a good idea to finish that book first and put this one on hold?"

"But I really want to read it," he whined.

"I know you do," I answered. "And I don't blame you. I've read it—and it's a really good book. But I'm really old and I've read lots of books. *I* even had to do a lot of work with this one."

"But all my friends are reading it," Dominic pouted.

"I know they are," I agreed. "But most of your friends have loved to read for a long time. They've read lots of long books already. You didn't like reading until recently, so you haven't read as much as they have. They have an easier time with Harry Potter because they've practiced more.

"How about if we make sure you get lots of practice with the things you'll need to be able to do well to read this book—and then as soon as you think you're really ready, we'll work through it together."

"But that could be a long time," he said, his eyes misting. "I want to read this now."

"Didn't your mom buy you this book?" I asked.

"Yeah," he said.

"Do you think she would be willing to sit down with you in the evenings and read it to you a little at a time?"

"Probably," he answered.

"Okay, then. You sit by her and look at the words while she reads. That will help you, too. You do that at home and we'll work here at school getting you to read lots of books that get harder all the time. Before you know it, you'll be ready to read a Harry Potter book all on your own. But in the meantime, let's get busy and practice."

Dominic's mother and I talked on the phone, and she was glad to help out at home. Dominic was now more motivated to be successful reading books at his correct level and definitely more willing to be guided to increasingly more difficult books. He was learning to be a reader.

Story Structure: The Basis of Questions About Fiction

If we truly want student readers like Dominic to lose themselves in imaginary worlds and identify with imaginary characters, we have to examine the strategies fiction readers use to make sense of the text. For readers to be engaged with texts, their purpose and that of the author must match. Fiction writers intend to pull readers into a world they have created—and the readers must plan to actually enter that world. Chapter 7 discussed the power of questions to propel readers' thinking forward, but for these questions to be effective they must match the genre the texts exemplify.

To ask effective questions when I'm reading fiction, I use my understanding of how story structure shapes the text. I remember that at the beginning of a book, the author introduces the characters, the setting, and the central problem. My questions must focus on these three key elements.

Once I know the problem, I always begin to question the characters' motivation to solve or cause that problem, the ways in which the events change the dynamics of the situation, and the changes the individual characters undergo. After the climax, my questions focus on how the change in the characters improve or further complicate their situations.

My instruction must help students understand that readers who choose fiction ask questions about fiction's key elements: the characters, the setting, the conflict, and the events. **Questions such as these move their reading forward:**

- How is this character important to the story?

- Why is this type of character necessary in this text?

- How will this character's choices be affected by his character traits?

- How do the relationships between the characters shape the decisions each makes?

- How does this setting shape the events in the text?

- What caused the characters' problems?

- How might these problems be solved?

These questions are very different from those generated by publishers and provided in teachers' editions or blackline master books. They are different from the questions my teachers asked me when I was in school and from those I asked students earlier in my career. Those questions drew from one person's understanding of the text and insisted that an entire group of readers match that narrow interpretation. But the students in my room bring their own experiences to the books they've chosen and their interpretations have value as well.

Meaningful questions come from readers themselves and not from an outside force uninvolved in the relationship developing between an individual reader and the author of a text. I don't want questions to provide proof a text has been read; I want these questions to make reading irresistible.

I use Jacquelyn Woodson's *The Other Side* as the anchor text for my minilesson when I teach how story structure shapes my thinking in a fictional narrative. This simple picture book about segregation has a clear plot structure that students can easily grasp.

I use the book for my minilessons two days in a row. On the first day, I introduce the plot map (see Chapter 6). Then, I read the book aloud, stopping at key points to talk about where the pages we have just read would fit on the map. The students and I identify the places in the text where exposition changes to rising action and where something happens to trigger a change that becomes the turning point. We then identify the events that serve as the falling action and determine the place in the text where the problem is actually resolved. Since this book is so beautifully written, it serves as a clear, comprehensible example of narrative structure.

As we determine where events from the story would fit on the plot map, I continually ask students, "Why do you think so?" I want them to tell me that the author is introducing the characters, setting, and problem in the exposition; that the identification of the problem begins the rising action; that the climax occurs when a change in a character or situation helps the reader see how the problem will be resolved; and that from that point to the actual resolution is the falling action. I want them to know readers expect this progression in a fiction text and use that knowledge to shape their reading.

On the second day, I use the map from the previous day to review plot structure and explain how knowledge of this map helps me understand fiction better. I say, "As a reader, I go into texts with expectations. When I read a fiction book, I use this plot map to help me know what to expect from the author at different points in the story. I know before I start that at the beginning of the book the author will provide details about the characters, the setting, and the problem—that's the author's job. My job as the reader, then, is to look for those details and use them to build an understanding of these fictitious people, where they are, and what problems they might face."

Together, the students and I look at the information Jacquelyn Woodson provides during the exposition in *The Other Side*. We learn two young girls, one black and one white, are the main characters. We learn the black child is telling the story. We learn both girls' names. We learn they live on the edge of town on neighboring plots of land and that a fence separates them. And we learn both girls have been taught they are never to go to the other side of the fence.

Too often, this is where teachers stop in their discussion of texts, particularly picture books. This is why when asked to generate questions on their own, students often offer pointless queries that can be answered with a single *yes* or *no*. Knowing the girls' names and their races (the characters) and that a fence in their small town separates them (the setting and problem) is not enough. Knowing details is the beginning of understanding, not the end.

Once the students have identified the characters, I say, "It's interesting to me that Jacquelyn Woodson uses two main characters, one white and one black. Why might she have done that?" This question causes the students to engage in the thinking that keeps dedicated readers reading—why do authors make the decisions they make while writing? What is their point? Woodson, of course, is focusing the reader on the reality of segregation, a belief system obviously advanced by the adults in the book and questioned by the two main characters. It is also significant that the young girl who refuses to let the fence separate her from the other children in the neighborhood is white, not black—a choice

Woodson makes, I'm sure, because if the black child had been the pushier one, the white society would never have accepted it.

Students can always identify the fence as the problem in the book—but the fence is just a symbol of the true problem, the small town's acceptance of segregation. I model deeper thinking by saying, "I know the problem is a fence that separates these children from each other—but as a reader I know that I always have to think past what the problem is and think about what caused it. Why might this fence be there?"

At this point, students clearly see someone has put up the fence to divide the races. I follow up with, "As a reader, I have to wonder—who would have done that? I don't think it would have been the children."

The students quickly realize the adults must have erected the fence. But, I want them to go beyond that detail to view the situation as thoughtful readers. Next I say, "I just can't stop thinking there. As a reader, I want to figure out what would make them do such a thing." This gets to the central issue represented both by the fence and by several events in the text. People in this town accept the thinking that has always been there—the races were meant to be separated—without ever questioning it. I intentionally repeat the phrase *as a reader* to identify what I do when I am functioning as a reader. These are the habits I will want my student readers to employ as well.

After discussing the deeper meaning of the picture book, I take time to remind my students that knowing plot structure helps shape my expectations for a text and also helps me think more deeply about the author's intended meaning. Just being able to draw a plot map and label and define its elements is very superficial knowledge that doesn't help students see how this knowledge can help them as readers.

◎ *Understanding Characters in Fiction Texts*

Character analysis is critical to readers of fiction. Readers must always analyze what kind of characters authors have created—and how their personalities shape the events of the plot. This is a skill I address every year.

When I plan a series of minilessons on character analysis, I first consciously identify what I do as a reader to determine what words I would use to describe a character. Then I teach these steps one at a time to my students. They need to know what a character is, what the difference is between a physical description and a character trait, what kinds of clues authors give about a character's personality, and how to look at these clues to determine what kind of person that particular character might be. They also need to know how readers use their understanding of characters to better understand the events, the problem, and the resolution.

Most students have spent great chunks of time deeply studying almost everything in the reading curriculum by the time they reach the intermediate grades. Reading is a global exercise—and the curriculum requirements don't change that much from year to year. What *does* change is the complexity of the texts in which the students are asked to apply what they have learned.

I am well aware that many students enter a grade without the prerequisite skills they should have. Poor instruction, processing difficulties, and family mobility are just a few of the problems that create this challenge for teachers. But before deciding everyone must be taught something as if it were a new skill, I always assess the understanding of the readers in the room. When students enter the middle school where I work, we assume that they have analyzed characters in the lower grades since our state curriculum requires teaching this skill beginning in fourth grade. But some students will have moved too much to have been anywhere for the deep teaching of this concept; some will have endured classrooms where the skill was poorly taught, and others still simply do not get it. But many of the students will have a working understanding, though not a mastery, of the idea of character analysis.

Since this is information I believe the majority of them already have, I do not supply definitions. Instead, I ask students questions to determine their core knowledge of the terms: *Who can tell me what a character is? What do readers mean when they talk about a character's traits? How do I decide what word best describes a character's personality?* If most of the students are unable to answer my basic questions, I scrap the plan for the day and start at the beginning. For this reason, I always have a short text ready to use for teacher modeling. As I read young adult literature, I collect short excerpts that offer clear examples of character development and keep them on file to use as the need arises. I always have this file ready—just in case.

But if the majority of my students can define the terms *character* and *character trait*, give me examples of character traits rather than physical descriptions, and list the types of clues authors give to establish the personalities of characters, we complete an anchor chart. The top of the chart defines the skill and the types of character clues authors use so that this information is readily available as a reminder when students need it. The rest of the chart is divided into three columns: *Character and Text, Clues from the Text,* and *Character Traits* (Figure 8–1). I expect the students to recreate this anchor chart in their readers' notebooks.

I use a text with which all the students are familiar, such as a fairy tale, popular movie, or text used as a read-aloud or shared reading. Together we collect the

Character Traits

A character trait is a noun or adjective used to describe the *behavior* of a particular person in a story.

Authors provide clues to a person's character in five specific ways: *descriptions, actions, reactions, conversations,* and *thoughts.*

Character and Text	Clues from the Text	Character Traits
Goldilocks from *The Three Bears*	Enters a house uninvited Helps herself to the food there Breaks furniture Takes a nap in someone else's bed	Rude, undisciplined, adventurous

Figure 8–1 *Anchor Chart on Character Traits*

clues and determine character traits. I stress that the clues collected must support the character traits we choose for each character. If I am currently using a single book as an anchor text, we use the characters from that book as our examples. We then discuss how creating a character with these traits affects the plot of the story.

After that, I turn students loose in the texts they have chosen to complete an identical graphic organizer analyzing one or more of the characters from their books. As I conduct deskside conferences, I ask them to explain how characters with these traits affected the plot's problem and solution.

When I teach a review minilesson like this, I am actually assessing the knowledge of my students. I don't need copies of a publisher-created test to do this. I watch for students whose expressions tell me they are confused; I remember whose answers showed me that they have a good grasp of this concept; and I make a mental note of students who may still have some confusion around a skill they are still developing. And then I plan lessons and conferences designed to meet the needs of the developing readers in my room.

◎ The Challenges of More Sophisticated Fiction

It was Bryan's second day reading Walter Dean Myers' *Autobiography of My Dead Brother,* and he was on page 24. This was a concern to me because he had been in the book for only about twenty minutes the day before, and we had just started our reading time that day. Fiction is continuous text, and I generally expect students to read about one page every three minutes, amounting to about ten pages in thirty minutes. He hadn't taken the book home, so he claimed to have read twenty-four pages in about thirty minutes. This seemed a little excessive to me.

"How's the book so far?" I asked.

"It's okay," he answered.

"That's not very enthusiastic," I responded. "Do you *like* the book?"

"It doesn't make any sense," he told me.

"Let's see if we can figure out what is confusing you. Do you think that part of the problem might be that you are reading too fast?" I suggested. "You've gone through this book pretty quickly."

"I read fast," he said.

"But it's not a race," I reminded him. "You don't have a deadline and you're not trying to beat someone else to the finish line. It isn't how long it takes you to read a book that's important. What's important is how well you understand it."

I turned back to the first page of the book, a page that begins with the words to the hymn "Precious Lord, Take My Hand"—written in italics and indented—and continues with the words of a minister conducting a funeral for fourteen-year-old Bobby Green, who we discover on page 4 was killed in a drive-by shooting. "What's happening here?" I asked, pointing to the song lyrics.

Bryan shrugged.

"Did you read this part?" I asked, pointing to the italicized song lyrics at the top of the page.

"I didn't even see it," he admitted. The formatting of the page had been new to him, and he had skipped straight to the first clear paragraph.

I asked him to start reading to me—and he read the words of the minister's sermon flawlessly, completely unaware of their meaning. He had absolutely no idea what he had just read. He had even ignored the black-and-white drawing on the facing page that showed a young man with eyes closed and arms crossed on his chest. The caption next to it read: "Bobby Green R. I. P."

"Bryan," I began, "let's take a minute to think about what is happening at the beginning of this book. Authors sometimes center text and put it in italics when they are quoting from something else, just the way Walter Dean Myers does here. These words are the words to a hymn called 'Precious Lord, Take My Hand.' Have you ever heard that song?"

"No, ma'am," he answered.

"It's one of my favorites because it was sung at my grandfather's funeral. In fact, it's sung at a lot of funerals. Now look at the drawing that begins this chapter. What do you think it is showing you?"

"It's a picture of a kid who's asleep," he answered.

"Are you sure he's asleep?" I asked.

"Well, his eyes are closed," he answered.

"Look carefully," I prompted. "What do you notice about his hands?"

"They're crossed across his chest," he said.

"And what is written next to him?"

Bryan read me the caption—and the light went on. "R. I. P.—that means *rest in peace*. This guy is *dead*!"

"Now does the beginning make sense?"

"Yea, this guy is dead—and that song is probably at his funeral."

Bryan was exactly right—but without realizing this important bit of information communicated both through Christopher Myers' drawing and through the words of a song and a sermon, he had read quickly through twenty-four pages of text, with which he truly wanted to be engaged, without any discernible comprehension. This text was, indeed, one that would help him grow—as long as I supported him with the new elements he would encounter in this more complex text.

◎ Dealing with Dialogue

One of the complications more sophisticated texts bring is understanding dialogue. Although students appreciate the amount of white space that large chunks of dialogue create in a text, they are very often confused when reading it. Sentences sometimes trail off unfinished with a series of little dots behind them, the identifying "he said" phrase often disappears, and sometimes quotations aren't finished at the end of a paragraph but continue on to the next with a new set of quotation marks. These are issues of convention that are crystal clear to proficient readers but that spark confusion as they are encountered by less skilled students.

Consider this passage from Jerry Spinelli's *Eggs*:

> Channel Ten News was showing a shabby-looking man in a scraggly gray beard and baggy pants standing on the corner of a busy intersection, waving. Smiling and waving. When the news went on to something else, John told them, "That was the Waving Man. I saw him myself in the city a couple of times."
>
> "What's he waving at?" said David.
>
> "The people driving by," said John. "He stands there every day during rush hour, waving at the cars. He waved at me once."
>
> "He does it every day?"
>
> "Far as I know."

"All year long? Even in the winter? When it's twenty degrees below zero?"

John nodded. "Always."

Primrose, who had been listening with increasing disbelief, said, "Why?"

John faced her. "Why does he wave?

"Yeah, why?"

John looked at the ceiling, and shrugged. "I don't know."

"Is he nutso?"

"No, I don't think so."

"So why does he do it?" (83–84)

There are three characters in this scene, and each talks at some point in time. Spinelli establishes that John and David are talking at first, but then eliminates markers identifying the speakers so that the dialogue will be read as a fast-paced conversation; the reader is expected to understand from the paragraphing and punctuation that John and David are taking turns talking. When a third character, Primrose, jumps into the conversation, Spinelli expects the reader to understand that the rest of the conversation is between only her and John; David is listening to them just as Primrose listened earlier. Once again, the speaker markers are eliminated. Developing readers often get confused by such common conventions and are unable to understand the ideas the dialogue is presenting both about the situation and the characters who are involved in it.

In order to help developing readers deal with dialogue effectively, instruction must teach them to:

- use the changing paragraphs to mark a change in speaker

- pay attention to the number of people involved in a conversation

- pay attention to names used in and around the conversation

- expect the speaker markers to disappear if there are only two people in the conversation

- understand that if a character has a long section of dialogue that requires more than one paragraph, each paragraph will begin with opening quotation marks—but the closing quotation marks will not come until the character stops talking.

Showing and discussing examples of these conventions from various trade books and watching for them in students' self-selected texts to be sure students are reading them effectively will help students master the skill of reading dialogue.

A Conference Around the Challenges of Dialogue

Mercy was reading "Satyagraha," a short story by Alden R. Carter in the collection *On the Fringe*. This particular day the minilesson had focused on how characters' conversations give clues to their personalities. I asked her to show me some dialogue in the text she was reading, just to verify that she recognized that quotation marks meant someone is talking. She pointed to the following passage:

> Bill Patchett spent his usual five minutes bashing his fists, forearms, and head into lockers. At six four, 240, that's a lot of frustration on the loose, and the rest of us stayed out of his way.
>
> "Hey, Bauer," he yelled at me. "Where were you on that last series?"
>
> I held up my bandaged hand. "Dislocated a finger."
>
> "And so little doc Ramdas wouldn't let you play, huh?"
>
> "It wasn't like that, Bill."

"Good job," I began. "How would you know right away that that was dialogue?"

"Well, there are lots of quotation marks," she replied.

Because she had not mentioned the paragraphing, I started my conference there. "When I look at this, I notice that there are really short paragraphs here—they don't even fill a whole line. Why would that be?"

No answer.

After the recommended amount of wait time, I knew that Mercy was still not clear on the fact that when writing dialogue authors must start a new paragraph every time the speaker changes. "Let's look at who's talking in each of these lines," I suggested. "Let's start with the first one. Where is the first bit of conversation?"

Mercy correctly identified the beginning of dialogue in the first paragraph. "Who is talking here?" I asked.

She had no idea.

In the next few minutes, we went line by line figuring out who was talking and how we would know that. We talked about paying attention to names before the conversation begins so that we can use them as clues to who's speaking. We talked about noticing when there is someone's name with commas around it in the dialogue itself because that gives you the name of the person being spoken to. We talked about the fact that authors sometimes drop speech markers when they are sure the reader can follow the dialogue without them, especially if they are trying to indicate a fast-paced conversation. We covered a lot of ground with a very short piece of text.

As an avid reader, I often take for granted the things I do automatically that actually present challenges for developing readers. As I uncover these challenges in deskside conferences, I am constantly reminded how important the small pieces are when I'm putting the big picture in place.

Detecting Point of View

Pronouns can confuse developing readers, particularly when texts are written from the first-person point of view. Unlike books written in third person that clearly state character names as they are introduced, books written in first person present readers with the challenge of discovering exactly who *I* might be.

In order to help developing readers understand point of view and consider its effects on the text, instruction must teach them to:

- pay attention to pronouns at the beginning of a book to determine if the story is being told from the viewpoint of the author (third-person point of view) or of one of the characters (first-person point of view)

- look for clues in the text to establish the identity of a first-person narrator

- understand why authors choose to tell their stories from a particular point of view

- look for formatting clues such as chapter titles, italics, or labeled borders that let the reader know that the narrator of a text has changed from one character to another

- realize that first-person point of view presents a biased picture of events and people in the text because everything is seen through one person's eyes and only that person's thoughts can be shared.

◎ *A Conference Around Point of View*

Jerry Spinelli's *Stargirl* is told in the first person by a narrator named Leo Borlock. Dominique, an often-combative girl who was repeating sixth grade, chose this book to read after I highlighted it in a booktalk in her class. I loaned her my own personal hardback copy—and she was thrilled.

I let Dominique read the first twenty pages or so before I held my first conference with her. She seemed to be totally engaged in a book for the first time all year, and I wanted to give her a chance to just enjoy herself before interrupting her train of thought. As always, I began the conference by asking her to tell me what was happening so far in her book. She enthusiastically began to retell the story as she understood it—but her understanding did not reflect the text as I remembered it.

The words in *Stargirl* were not difficult for Dominique—but the first-person narrative had left her confused about many of the key elements of the plot. She had missed the one vague reference to the narrator's name in the prologue—and her inability to identify this key character was compromising her understanding.

"Dominique," I began, "I think you have a couple of details mixed up, which sometimes happens to all of us when we read. Let's start at the beginning. Who is the main character?"

"Stargirl," she smiled.

"And what other characters are important?"

"Kevin," she answered, referring to the narrator's best friend.

"Yes," I acknowledged. "And anyone else?"

Her brow furrowed as she tried to remember other characters' names. "No one that I really think is important," she answered. She was clearly not understanding that the person telling the story was himself a very key character in it.

"Dominique," I began, "have you ever heard the term *narrator* before?"

"I think so," she answered.

"Do you know what it means?" I asked.

"Not really," she replied

"Sometimes authors decide that the best way to tell a story is through the eyes of a character. This character is called the narrator."

I quickly grabbed a Ramona Quimby book off the nearby bookshelf and showed her how Beverly Cleary uses third-person pronouns such as *she* to refer to Ramona. "This is called third-person point of view because it uses what are called third-person pronouns such as *he* and *she* to tell the story," I explained. "Beverly Cleary decided when she wrote this that she as the author was the best one to tell the story. This makes the author the observer who is reporting what is happening to the reader. It allows the author to show you the events and characters in a sort of neutral way. The only time you will see words like *I* and *me* in a book like this is in dialogue. They'll always be inside quotations marks."

Then we went to the first page of *Stargirl*. "Now let's look at the very first sentence in *Stargirl*," I said, turning to the prologue on page one. "*When I was little, my uncle Pete had a necktie with a porcupine painted on it*," I read.

"Did you notice the words *I* and *my* in that sentence?" I asked.

"Yes," she said.

"Those are called first-person pronouns because they refer to the person who is actually talking. Jerry Spinelli decided when he wrote this book that he wanted a character to tell the story so that you as the reader could see all the people and events through that person's eyes. That person then becomes the narrator. The reader then becomes like a friend who is sitting and listening to this person tell the story."

"Oh, I get it!" she said enthusiastically. "Stargirl is telling the story!"

Dominique was a student with no reading confidence, so I didn't want to diminish her enthusiasm—but I did need to redirect her thinking. "Well, she certainly *could* tell the story! She's an interesting person, isn't she?"

"She is really weird!" Dominique laughed.

"One of our jobs as readers when we read a book told by a narrator is to figure out who that narrator is. The author's job is to find a way to help make the narrator's identity clear. Let's read a little farther through this first part and see if we can figure out who *I* is."

"It's Stargirl—I just told you," Dominique argued.

"It might be," I nodded. "But I have to find something in the text itself that tells me for sure who the narrator is. The author gets to pick who tells the story, not the reader. Our job as readers is to ask ourselves who is telling the story—and to read on with this question in our heads until it is answered. Why don't you read to me—and stop when you get to the part where Jerry Spinelli lets us know who *I* is in this story."

The fourth paragraph of *Stargirl* gives the narrator's name. It reads:

> On my fourteenth birthday, I read about myself in the local newspaper. The family section ran a regular feature about kids on their birthdays, and my mother had called in some info. The last sentence read: "As a hobby, Leo Borlock collects porcupine neckties."

Dominique read right over it without stopping—and went on to paragraph five.

"Stop just a second," I said. "Let me read you that last paragraph again—and you tell me if you can figure out who is telling this story."

I read the paragraph again, even emphasizing Leo's name. Still no response from Dominique.

"Pronouns can be tricky," I began, "but they are very important to us as readers as we try to gather information about characters and events in a story. Let's look more carefully at this paragraph. Whose birthday is it?"

"Stargirl's," Dominique insisted.

"How do you know that?" I asked.

"Because this book is called *Stargirl*. She must be telling the story."

This sort of logic is very common with developing readers—and the reason their comprehension often breaks down. They want things to be the way they want them to be—and they often ignore textual information that would clarify their thinking. They don't understand that readers are always open to changing their minds based on new information from the author.

"You know, when I started reading this book and saw the word *I* in the first sentence, I thought Stargirl would be telling the story, too. I mean, her name is the title of the book and the first sentence says *I*. So I read those first few paragraphs just like you, assuming that Stargirl was the one who had been given the porcupine necktie. But then I read that fourth paragraph and changed my mind. What do you think I saw in that fourth paragraph that let me know that Stargirl *wasn't* telling the story—someone else was?"

Dominique looked frustrated. "I don't know," she mumbled.

I dropped my head down to the level of Dominique's eyes and continued. "Part of the fun of reading is trying to predict what an author will do and seeing if you're right—and the best authors, like Jerry Spinelli, always find ways to surprise us. I love it when an author does something I wasn't expecting. It doesn't mean I'm a bad reader—just that the author is a really clever writer!

"Talk to me a little about this fourth paragraph," I prompted, "because Spinelli put this paragraph here on purpose to let you as a reader know who was going to be telling the story. Don't use *any* character's name just yet—what is the paragraph about?"

Dominique reluctantly went back to the text. "It's about her fourteenth birthday," she answered.

"Do we know yet from what the author has said—not what we think is right—that it is a *girl's* fourteenth birthday?"

Dominique suddenly sat up in her chair. "No, but I think it's Stargirl's," she said.

"But you have to be able to prove it. Do you know for sure from what the author has said that it is a girl's birthday?"

"No," she admitted.

"Okay," I continued, "so it's *someone's* birthday—but we're not sure whose, though we think it might be Stargirl's, right?"

"Right," she said.

"Now let's keep reading," I said. We read the second sentence and stopped. "What new information did that sentence add?"

"That her mother sent the stuff into the paper," Dominique answered.

"*Her* mother?" I laughed.

"Okay, *someone's* mother," she answered.

I read the last sentence. "Do you notice the quotation marks in this sentence?" I asked.

"Yeah," she answered.

"Why are those there?"

"Because someone is talking," she said.

"Usually that's why we use quotation marks," I replied. "But we also use them if we copy someone else's writing word for word. This sentence quotes the last sentence in the newspaper article. That's why the quotation marks are there. So what did the newspaper article say?"

Dominique read me the quotation.

"And who sent that sentence in to the newspaper?"

"*Someone's* mother," she replied sarcastically.

"*Whose* mother?" I asked. "Read that sentence again."

Suddenly the light went on. "Leo Borland's mother," she laughed.

"So who is the narrator?"

"Leo Borland?" she answered "A *boy* is telling this story?"

"That's right," I replied.

"Then I need to start over. I've been reading this all wrong," she said.

And start over she did. In our conferences through the rest of the book, she continually understood both the characters and events and the point Spinelli was trying to make about popularity and conformity. She finished the book in two weeks, taking it home every night to read—something she had never done before, she said. She went on to read other Spinelli books, but at the end of the school year she told me that *Stargirl* would always be her favorite book. It was the first one she had ever read all the way through.

Many books written for young people are written from the first-person point of view. Some, like Wendelin Van Draanen's *Flipped*, use alternating points of view to tell a story from different angles. Readers of this text must be sophisticated enough to realize that *different* people become *I* in alternating chapters. They must be flexible enough in their thinking to gather sometimes conflicting information presented from differing points of view—and use this information to form fully developed pictures of the characters and their situations.

Supporting Readers of Fiction

As students leave the comfort of picture books and move into novels, we must anticipate their challenges and teach ahead of their need. Well-crafted mini-lessons and deskside conferences can help these readers thrive as consumers of stories that whisk them away. Our lessons and conferences could hold the key to the door of lifelong reading.

Questions for Reflection

To become lifelong readers, students must learn the power of a good story to transport them to places that exist only in the imagination. But they will first need to learn how to work through the challenges sophisticated fiction texts can present. As you plan lessons to help your students become better fiction readers, consider these questions:

- Do your students understand the importance of using story structure to shape their expectations for fiction texts? What minilessons might you create to address the elements of a story?

- When you offer minilessons on reading dialogue, how might you assure yourself students are understanding it fully? Which kids need reteaching?

- Can you work with a group of other teachers to start files of short texts that you can use to teach the demands of fiction?

Teaching Comprehension in Nonfiction Texts

esterday one of my teachers stopped me in the hallway and said, "You *have* to go to your computer and read your email!"

"Okay," I said. "But why?"

"I just had our librarian take a picture of my kids in the library and email it to you. You have to see it to believe it." She then named five boys whose names everyone in the school knew (never a good thing). These boys had just spent forty-five minutes in the library glued to the newest edition of *Guinness World Records*.

"We couldn't get them away from the book!" she giggled. "*Those* boys! I stayed the whole period in the library just because they were so involved in *reading*!"

This is not an unusual occurrence, but one that continually surprises many teachers. Even the most reluctant reader can often be tempted by books full of pictures and interesting facts. Nonfiction is often my most effective tool for engaging students in reading. Curiosity is what drives all of us, including our students, to read nonfiction.

By limiting the reading students do in my classroom to fiction, I fail to show them that *books* have the answers to their questions. In an age when quick answers can be found on the Internet, students will never learn to immerse themselves in a topic and build a depth of knowledge if I never give them time to explore nonfiction texts and support them as they learn to work through them.

Bridging to Informational Texts

I live in the fourth largest city in the country. Like all other cities, Houston has hundreds of buildings of varying shapes and sizes. I certainly recognize an office building when I see one, but that doesn't mean I'll have an easy time navigating my way through it. I recently had to deliver some papers to an insurance office that was in a high-rise building not far from my school. First there was the challenge of the parking lot—would it be behind the building, under it, across the street? Once I found that, there was the challenge of where I was allowed to park, certainly not in the contract-parking-only spaces. Then there was the challenge of navigating from the parking lot to the actual building since several buildings shared the same parking facility. That accomplished, there was finding the correct floor for the insurance office followed by the search for the elevator. Once I found it and rode it to the correct floor, I had to figure out which way to turn to find the office I was looking for. All this confusion—and I am *familiar* with office buildings!

Students recognize a book when they see one, but that doesn't mean they know how to navigate their way through it. If students have spent the majority of their time reading fiction, when they choose an informational text they experience the same level of confusion that I feel in strange office buildings. These books don't follow the narrative structure these students have come to expect from texts.

When students encounter nonnarrative informational texts, they enter the text looking for characters and setting, but there are none to be found. They expect a story arc they won't find. They encounter unfamiliar print conventions such as headings, chapter titles, and call-outs. What are fiction readers to do?

Without using informational texts in minilessons and encouraging students to read them, we are isolating them from important skills that will serve them well in both their academic and their personal lives. It may be unfamiliar territory for us at first, but it is vitally important that we allow—and even encourage—our students to choose informational texts to read.

Understanding the Purpose of Nonfiction Texts

It is important for students to realize that the books found in the nonfiction section are often just as different from one another as they are from fiction. Biographies follow a narrative structure much like fiction, but the author's primary purpose is to relate information about a significant person, not to create an imaginary world. Well-written biographies will make the people on whom they are centered unforgettable—but the authors are limited to the realities of these people's lives and cannot embellish them with fascinating, fictional details. Biographies are read to learn more about real people and how the events of their lives shaped their futures. Readers reading biographies must have different expectations from those reading novels.

The purpose of informational texts is to provide information about selected topics. They offer readers a chance to explore these topics deeply. I worry sometimes about the power of the Internet to actually limit our knowledge. If I have a question, I can just type it into a search box on the computer, and I will instantly be guided to the answer. But an informational text will answer that question and so many more.

I want my students to learn to take their time and immerse themselves in a topic of interest, not just quickly read three or four lines and think they know about infectious diseases or what killed the dinosaurs. I want them to develop curiosity, not collect factoids. For all of these reasons, I want them to understand what to expect from informational books.

I begin conferences with readers of nonfiction just like I begin those with fiction readers, by asking, "What genre is this book?" and "What do you know to expect from this genre?" I hope to hear the student tell me something besides, "It's nonfiction." Instead, I want them to identify whether it is a narrative or informational text.

The best way I have found to help students understand this important distinction is to bring in stacks of trade books and have them generate their own ideas for how to distinguish between a narrative and informational text. To spare them from having to wrestle with such sophisticated words, I tell them I want to recognize the difference between nonfiction that tells a story and nonfiction that gives information. I also caution them that nothing is true *all* the time; we are just looking for general patterns. Having them generate this list allows them to truly own the distinctions. (See Figure 9–1 for an example.)

I explicitly teach the difference between these two types of nonfiction in mini-lessons. During these lessons, I coach my students to answer my genre question with statements such as, "It's a biography, so it will tell the story of a person's life in time order." Or, "It's informational text. It's going to give me interesting information about snakes, but it won't be like a story." When I have taught them to

Story	Information
• Has a lot of short paragraphs because it includes conversations	• Usually divides up the text with subtitles and headings
• Often uses only a person's first name	• Usually uses a person's whole name or just their last name
• Relies mostly on words to give information	• Includes a lot of graphics (maps, charts, diagrams, pictures) that give information
• Organizes the information in time order	• Organizes the information by topic
• Usually doesn't use bold-faced words	• Puts words in boldfaced type if they are important

Figure 9–1   *Student-Generated Differences Between Narrative and Informational Texts*

articulate what to expect from the nonfiction books they have chosen, I have made them stronger readers.

The Power of Pictures

The Scholastic warehouse in Houston holds a half-price book sale twice a year—I live for these sales! Last year my principal was kind enough to give me several hundred dollars to spend at the December sale—and spend it I did! Since the nonfiction collection in our literacy center is not what I would like it to be, I bought a significant number of nonfiction texts.

The book that swept the school by storm was *Hot Cars Cool Rides* by Marty Padgett. Its pages are covered with full-color pictures of just what the title says—hot cars! We still cannot keep enough copies of this book and others like it in our classrooms—and when books disappear, these are always the first to go. Pictures engage kids, and we need to use that to our advantage.

Pictures drew Isaac in. Since he is a notoriously reluctant reader, I was surprised one day to find him hopelessly engaged in a book. The book was filled with close-up pictures of snakes and toads and roaches and all manner of vermin—and these were *some* pictures! As I looked over his shoulder, I was greeted with a picture of a disgusting-looking insect that I did not recognize.

"What in the world is that?" I asked.

"I'm not sure, miss," he answered. "Pretty gross, huh?"

"You got that right!" I laughed. "Is there anything there to tell us what it is?" Immediately he went to the text, read it, and gave me the name of the hideously disgusting critter in the photograph. I have blocked that name and the title of the book from my memory—but I did say to the student, "Great job! You knew to look at the words near the picture to find out what it was."

"Yeah, miss," he said, glued to the page. "And right here it even talks about how it eats. It's pretty cool—wanna hear?"

I have been teaching middle school long enough to know that when a boy wants to tell me something "pretty cool" about how a disgusting-looking creature eats, I should pass. But the conference with this student reminded me that books with engaging pictures will pull students to the text. There may be fewer words in these books—but the ones that are there will capture and hold students' attention. And these books can be useful tools in engaging my most reluctant readers.

As these readers learn books can be filled with fascinating details, I can gradually move them from such picture-driven books to ones that rely more on words. I can help them learn to use the words in the texts to make their own visual images. And I can help them discover that longer, more text-driven texts provide them with a deeper understanding of topics that fascinate them.

Reading Informational Texts

Several years ago I accompanied a class to the library and came back to their classroom afterwards to help with deskside conferences. One of the boys had gotten an informational text filled with pictures and was gleefully thumbing through the pages, stopping when a picture caught his eye and reading the caption under it. Furious, his teacher crossed the classroom, turned to the first page of the book, and told him in no uncertain terms that he was to start on the first page and read the book the way it was supposed to be read—one page at a time from front to back.

I will never contradict a teacher in front of her students, and I know that this woman meant well. But the truth is that informational texts do *not* have to be read from front to back in order. Readers can skip around in them all they want and never even read parts that don't interest them. The text in most informational books is not continuous as it is in narrative texts. I teach my students that distinction and allow them to read nonnarrative nonfiction the way it is read in the real world.

Due to its topic-driven structure, I need to take the time in minilessons to show my students how the table of contents and index in an informational text work. These characteristics are seldom, if ever, found in fiction. These features of nonfiction texts help a reader know if the book they are considering will answer the questions that are driving them toward these books in the first place.

Nonfiction Conferences

Just as in conferences around novels, the questions I ask students who are reading nonfiction texts center around the demands of the genre. I direct them to notice the elements of nonfiction texts that are intentionally placed there to help them as readers.

I ask questions that coach students to notice conventions such as captions, charts, and timelines. I recommend they preview each chapter by looking at the pictures and graphics and using the headings to generate questions. Every word I say to nonfiction readers is aimed at increasing their curiosity and hunger for more nonfiction texts. (See Figures 9–2 and 9–3 for suggested questions and teaching points for nonfiction conferences.)

Conference Questions for Nonfiction Texts

What did you already know about this topic before you started reading?

This question helps me determine whether the reader already has so much background knowledge that the book is not adding to what is known and is thus too easy and will not help the reader grow.

What can you learn from looking at the graphics on this page?

This question helps readers know that they should pay attention to these graphics as they read.

What does this heading prepare you to learn from this next section of reading?

This question prompts the reader to expect specific types of new information from the text.

Why do you think this word is written in boldface type?

This question helps readers understand that boldfaced words are those that the author thinks the reader might not know because they are specialized vocabulary particular to the topic. These words are usually defined in the text itself, in a gloss on the page, or in a glossary at the back of the book. The meaning of these words will often provide new learning.

What is something interesting the author told you about this topic?

This reminds readers that a nonfiction author's job is to interest the reader as well as to provide information. Well-written nonfiction books often contain many more details than textbooks because the authors intentionally collect information they think will engage readers of the text.

Figure 9–2 *Conference Questions for Nonfiction Texts*

Teaching Points for Conferences on Nonfiction

- Biographies have a narrative structure much like fiction but have a different purpose, namely to show how events in a real person's life shaped his or her future.

- Informational text is organized around a topic and presents facts about that topic to deepen readers' understanding.

- Nonfiction texts include graphics that are meant to provide further information—and these graphics should not be skipped.

- The chapter titles, headings, and subheadings in nonfiction texts are there to guide readers to the type of information provided.

- Nonfiction texts contain specialized vocabulary that is used only when talking about the topic under discussion, so the reader may never have encountered these words before.

- Readers must expect these unknown words to be somehow related to the topic and use this expectation to help them determine the meaning from context.

- Authors of nonfiction texts often define words they think the reader won't know either directly in the text, in glosses on the side of the page, or in glossaries at the back of the book.

- Informational books are written in a much more engaging way than textbooks because their purpose is more than to just give vast quantities of information—it is to fascinate the reader.

- Information in a nonfiction book is organized according to the author's purpose. The most common purposes are to describe something, to explain how one thing caused another, to show a sequence of events, or to detail a problem and how it was or might be solved.

- Authors usually employ a variety of text structures throughout the book, each chosen to meet the purpose of that particular section of text.

Figure 9 3 *Teaching Points for Nonfiction Conferences*

The True Meaning of K-W-L

Almost all of my conferences with nonfiction readers rely in some way on Donna Ogle's (1986) K-W-L (Know-Want to Know-Learned) strategy. This powerful strategy has too often been misunderstood and poorly implemented. Its purpose is to help student readers access their prior knowledge and generate questions before reading to deepen their understanding of the text. It combines three proficient reader strategies: activating schema, questioning, and synthesizing (Keene and Zimmermann 2007; Harvey and Goudvis 2007). But its misuse in classrooms has made students see it as a teacher-directed activity that generates decorations for the walls of the classroom and has no personal meaning for them as readers.

When I work with student readers who are challenged by nonfiction texts, I rely on the basics of the K-W-L strategy to guide student thinking. I want the *students* to own this strategy—so I ask them questions such as

- What did you already know about the topic of this book?

- What made you decide to read a book on that topic since you already had some knowledge about it?

- What about this particular book made you choose it from all the other books in that section?

- What did you think you would learn from this book to add to what you already knew?

I want the students to understand that readers choose nonfiction texts about topics in which they are interested. Often they already have a great deal of knowledge about the topic, but they still have unanswered questions and want to learn more. They often discover in the course of the reading that new information changes their thinking about topics they thought they knew.

This was my experience two summers ago when I read Nathaniel Philbrick's *Mayflower*. I already knew that the original colonists came to America aboard a ship named the *Mayflower*—and I knew some of their names. I knew they had had problems that prompted them to draw up an agreement called the Mayflower Compact. I knew they had been poorly prepared for life on a new continent and had had to rely on the natives for help to prevent starvation. I did not know that many of those first colonists had already left England and gone to the Netherlands to practice their religion or that many of the people who organized the first trips to the New World were borderline scoundrels who were duping the prospective colonists. I did not know that some of the colonists actually stole food from the natives who had tried to help them. In fact, there was a great deal I did not know. Reading that book changed my view of the earliest events in my country's history and of the people who had often been misrepresented in the books I had read as a child. It deepened my knowledge and changed my thinking. That is what I expect from nonfiction—and why I often choose to read it.

I share examples such as this from my own reading as I work with students who have chosen nonfiction texts. They need to be clear about their reasons for choosing the books they hold—and they must be curious enough to have questions and expect them to be answered. They must expect the new information they encounter to change their thinking in some way.

By asking students to talk about what they already know, to wonder about what new information they will encounter, and to verbalize what new information they have learned, I have—without a three-column chart—asked students to use K-W-L as a strategy. By repeatedly focusing on these three strategies as I work with nonfiction readers, I help them learn to own them and to use them without prompting to deepen their comprehension of nonfiction texts.

Expecting New Learning

The *L* in K-W-L stands for *learned*, as "What Did You Learn?" Students who have chosen nonfiction texts should approach them from what Rosenblatt (1965, 1978, 2005) calls an *efferent stance*, an expectation that they will learn something from what they are about to read and carry that new knowledge with them. This is, after all, the reason why skilled readers choose nonfiction books in the first place. It is imperative that student readers internalize this expectation and use it to guide their reading of both biographies and informational texts.

Like my student readers, I choose to read nonfiction books on topics that interest me. For nearly all of my career, I have taught in Title I schools with high immigrant populations, so Rubén Martínez's book *The New Americans*, based on the 2004 PBS series of the same name, caught my eye. Recent immigrants from five different countries are interviewed in the book, each explaining why they came to the United States and what their joys and challenges have been here. In the fifth chapter, titled "India to Silicon Valley: Anjan Bacchu," I read this fact: "The International Council on Education estimates that nearly half of the country's [India's] newly graduated engineers and scientists go abroad for work. . . . It is perhaps the greatest emigration in India's history" (188). I didn't know that!

That is the phrase I want my students to own—*I didn't know that*! And I want them to own it with an exclamation point at the end—new learning should be exciting!

I start an anchor chart with this exclamation as the title and model its use by putting a bullet and writing, "Half of the young engineers and scientists in India leave the country." I explicitly discuss the importance of putting what I learned into my own words to show that I truly understand it. I am not copying word for word; I own the information. Then I ask students to create a similar chart in their readers' notebooks.

"I want you to learn something new from your reading today," I say. "In fact, I want you to learn lots of new things. I will give you five sticky notes to mark places where you learn something new. If you need more, just ask. Then at the end of reading time you can add what you learned to your chart.

"You may get so excited about what you learned that you want to write something down right away rather than mark it with a sticky note and come back to it later. That's fine—if you want to hold that idea immediately, knock yourself out!"

If I see students reading who are using no sticky notes and have nothing written on their charts, I know it is time for a conference. Sometimes the problem is that the student has so much background knowledge that he has not learned anything new. In that case, he has chosen a book that doesn't meet his demands as a reader. Nonfiction readers need to learn something new to make their reading worthwhile. Sometimes the problem is that a student is not noticing when she learns something new because she hasn't learned to expect it. In that case, I go back to the nearest heading and read until *I* learn something new and point it out. Then I ask her to do the same thing. As soon as she identifies new learning and marks it, I move on to another conference. Once in a while, the problem is that a student has chosen a book too far above her current reading abilities. Just as I do when such readers are reading fiction, I help them make a better book choice. By creating an expectation they will learn something new, I am supporting the developing readers in my classroom as they learn to navigate through nonfiction as well as fiction texts.

Deepening Knowledge: The Basis of Questions About Nonfiction

Like fiction readers, readers of nonfiction need to generate questions that will push them forward through the text. These questions should honor the genre around which they are formed. I need to teach my students that the questions they ask about nonfiction are tied to the knowledge this genre provides. **Some questions that have worked include:**

- How does what I already know about this subject shape my expectations for this text?

- What information given by the author connects to what I already know and deepens my understanding?

- What did I learn that I didn't know before?

- What information given by the author changes what I thought I knew about this topic?

- What did the author consider to be the most important information to share on this topic—and do I agree?

- What, if any, propaganda techniques is the author using to try to redirect my thinking on this topic?

Reading nonfiction expands our understanding of the world. Questions such as these shape those new understandings.

Broadening the Vision of Reading

The idea of having students reading both fiction and nonfiction texts in the classroom may seem daunting. But the truth is that students will love what they love. Some will crave time to be lost in the imaginary worlds that fiction writers create. Others would rather spend their time becoming masters of the real world in which they live. If my goal is to lead my students to a lifelong love of reading, I need to broaden their vision of reading as well as my own, and create places for every kind of book in their reading worlds.

Questions for Reflection

Helping students grow as independent readers means encouraging them to read across a wide range of texts, including nonfiction. As you think about helping students learn to comprehend these texts, ask yourself:

- What's your collection of nonfiction texts like? Does it need a makeover? Are you familiar with the collection available in the library at your school?

- Will you be comfortable having to vary responses for your readers, allowing some to respond to fiction and others to nonfiction?

- Can you work with a group of other teachers to start files of short texts that you can use to teach the demands of nonfiction?

10

Assessing Independent Readers

A t the end of every school year, my district sends me a database with the
state reading test scores of all the fifth graders who will be entering our
middle school the next year. From this information, we know who passed
the test and who didn't. The only problem is we don't know *why*. It is not until
the students actually enter our classrooms and we work with them every day that
we begin to understand the individual challenges each reader faces.

Assessment has earned a bad reputation in the past few years as state and
national governments have blurred the line between assessment and evalua-
tion. In my practice, I think of assessment in the purest educational sense of
the word—an effort by a professional educator to look at individual students
and see where their strengths and weaknesses lie. For years, educators' mantra
has been that assessment should drive instruction. In an independent reading
classroom, it does.

Reading Response

One of my most important assessment tools is the daily reading response, which allows me to continually assess the progress of individual readers. These responses will be ineffective, however, unless they benefit the students as well by becoming a vehicle for extending their thinking.

During independent reading time, I am teaching *reading*, not writing. Writing ability often lags behind reading development (Bear, Invernizzi, Templeton, and Johnston 2003), and students' lack of ability to express themselves in writing should not skew my view of the thinking these students are actually doing as readers. For this reason, I have found graphic organizers to be better responses than open-ended questions. In a time not set aside for supported independent reading, I use open-ended questions to teach written response to texts—and the students use their graphic organizer notes as prewriting.

The ultimate goal is to have students personally connect with what they are reading and respond in what Rosenblatt (1978) terms either an aesthetic or an efferent way. Aesthetic responses ask readers to emotionally connect with a text while efferent responses ask students to focus on information gained from the reading.

◎ *Notes, Not Worksheets*

I was behind a teacher at the copy machine one day and watched as he ran and assembled a packet of materials for his students to complete. He copied every page of a blackline master book of activities for the book he was planning to teach—page after page of vocabulary activities, crossword puzzles, and comprehension questions. The pages were collated, stapled, and ready for distribution. The students would be very busy for the next few weeks.

So, what is wrong with this approach? When teachers rely on blackline master books, they are allowing publishers who have never met their students to determine what is important. They also allow the publishers to choose texts worth teaching. After all, if there is no blackline master book, how can they possibly teach the text? Harste and Leland (2007) remind us that "curriculum is too important to be left in the hands of those who rarely come in contact with students" (9).

Students will be more engaged in their reading and will develop greater reading proficiency if *they* are given the responsibility for determining what is important in the texts they are reading and are allowed to develop and support their own interpretation of texts (Rosenblatt 1978, 2005; Langer 1995; Aukerman 2006). If I expect my students to actively construct meaning, I must support them by modeling ways to engage with texts and to hold their thinking. Then, if I monitor their responses to know who needs more help with comprehension, my students' reading and thinking abilities can grow.

If teachers continue to rely on published materials written by people who have never met the students in their classroom, they risk greatly limiting the directions in which their students can grow. More important, they are causing students to associate reams of worksheets with the act of reading, an association not likely to lead to the development of lifelong readers. On the other hand, real-world readers use strategies to skillfully read texts they have chosen and in which they are truly engaged. All this happens at an unconscious level unless they have learned, as Keene and Zimmermann (2007) illustrate, how to be metacognitive readers. Students need to understand the kinds of thinking their teachers do as readers that make reading enjoyable.

Teaching students to organize their thinking with graphic organizers is very different from supplying students with blackline copies to use. The goal is to have the *students* own the strategy, not to have them depend on a teacher to provide them with a copied organizer, which becomes a glorified worksheet. Students need to learn the value and versatility of two- and three-column charts, lists, and webs and to devise their own ways of using these for effective note taking. If someone else draws the graphic for them and runs them a copy, students are merely filling in the blanks. By drawing and labeling the organizers themselves, they are focusing on the type of thinking they will need to do to be successful and competent readers.

◎ Choosing the Target

I must carefully choose the skill or strategy I want to teach students. By directing students' attention to a specific target that will focus their reading efforts for the day, I am also controlling the quality of students' reading. Organized notes can focus on one of three areas: engagement, skills, or strategies. All are important, and the notes assigned to students should represent a balance between these three areas.

I consider several things when choosing a focus for the day's notes:

- Am I more concerned about students' engagement with their texts or their understanding of them?

- What have I already taught in enough depth that I feel my students can apply to their own reading?

- What kinds of texts are my students reading?

- Will one organizer work for the entire class or do I need to individualize more?

- How far are my students ready for me to push their thinking?

- Have I modeled what effective notes might look like with examples from my own reading during minilessons?

Organizers that target engagement look at how involved the students are in their texts and invite them to connect with or critique their reading. These organizers can also help readers think about their own reading—how they choose texts or how they overcome distractions. When students begin a new book, for example, I often ask them to make a list of what they expect from the text before they begin reading. Then for a few days, their response focuses on whether their expectations are being met—or if the text has prompted new expectations.

Organizers targeting strategies focus on the tools proficient readers use to comprehend what they read (Keene and Zimmermann 2007; Harvey and Goudvis 2007). But these strategies are a means to an end, not an end in themselves. Organizers focused on strategies help students learn to apply these tools to their own reading in order to better understand what they read.

Strategic readers know how to distinguish important from supplementary ideas. If I want to be sure students are correctly identifying the important elements in their own self-selected texts, I have students create a two-column chart with the left-hand column labeled *What I Read* and the right-hand column labeled *Why It's Important*. This organizer works with both fiction and nonfiction texts.

Organizers targeting skills help me gauge where each student is in the course of developing the overall abilities proficient readers gain through strategy use. Educators have given these abilities labels and devised ways of testing them, all in an effort to determine whether or not readers are competent. But in the real world, people don't label these skills—they just exhibit them. If I want to be sure students can identify main ideas and their supporting ideas, I might assign a web as the response, modeling how to use it in a minilesson with nonfiction texts. If I want to be sure they are aware of the context clues that help them with unfamiliar words, I might ask them to make a three-column chart with the word and page number, clues to the meaning from the text, and their guess of the definition, modeling this with a short text as well. By reviewing the student responses, I can determine which students need more help in mastering these essential reading skills.

Once I have assigned a particular graphic organizer as a reading response, responsibility for use of that organizer moves to the students. They must use these simple graphics to make their thinking around targeted skills or strategies visible so that I can assess their understanding or confusion. I expect student errors and see them as opportunities for student growth, not weaknesses in my instruction.

By assessing how each individual reader applies what has been taught, I can begin to understand the challenges facing each reader. And by addressing these individual confusions in one-on-one deskside conferences, I can target my instruction to meet the needs of every student in the room.

Assessing Reading Responses

Because I expect to discover errors in thinking, I *must* check student reading responses regularly. I have found the best way to do this is at the student's desk as I stop for a deskside conference. If I am looking at these without the student present, I can often make wrong assumptions about a student's thinking. What looks like lack of effort may actually be sincere confusion. Only a conversation with the student will help me understand the responses.

Maria is a case in point. There is not a sweeter child in the entire classroom. She greets me with a smile every day, always wants a quick hug, and has not been off task for one second of the entire school year. She logs in her reading log, reads the entire thirty minutes each day, and always completes her response graphic without reminder. But her responses tell the story—Maria is just not getting it.

This particular day Maria was reading *Ramona the Pest* by Beverly Cleary. We had been working on making inferences and she was to use a three-column chart: what the text said, what she knew that linked to that, and the inference that resulted from that link.

Maria was smiling as she read that day, seemingly enjoying every word Beverly Cleary had set down on the page. I pulled up next to her and said, "You're smiling, Maria! You must really be enjoying this book."

"I am, Mrs. Allison," she said. "It's a really good book."

"Can you tell me what's been happening so far?"

"Well, Ramona is having a party and she's inviting a bunch of kids from her class."

"Sounds interesting. Have you made any inferences while you were reading?"

"Oh, yeah," she nodded, still smiling. "I've made a lot already."

"Great!" I said. "Could you share one with me?"

"Well, right here it says that Ramona's mom said she could have a party. That's what the text says. So I know that when moms say you can have a party, you can have a party. So my inference is that she's going to have a party."

Obviously there's a party in Ramona's future—but just as obviously, Maria is totally off course on what it means to make an inference. She has part of the formula down—an inference is putting something from the text with something in your head. The part she *doesn't* get is that this mixture of information is supposed to result in a new idea that isn't anywhere on the page.

"Wow!" I said, stalling for time. "I can tell that you understand that to make an inference you have to combine the words on the page with something you know in your head. Let me see the inferences you made yesterday."

Just as I suspected, every inference she had made—and she had filled a page with them—took something on the page and basically restated it two more times, once in the column where she was to put what prior knowledge she had used and once more in the column for the actual inference. If this response had shown up on a stack of papers taken home for grading, I might think Maria was just being lazy and going through the motions. By asking her to show me her responses and talk me through them, I understood that she thought she was making true inferences. The problem wasn't lack of effort, but of understanding.

"Maria," I said. "I think there's an important piece of inferring that you may not have understood when we talked about it in class—and that is my fault, not yours. Did you realize that an inference is something that is never actually written in the book? It is an idea the author wants you to make all on your own from the clues she gives you in the text. Your job as a reader is to find the clues, put them together with things you know in your head, and figure out what the author is trying to tell you."

Maria gave me a blank stare, obviously saddened by her perception that she had disappointed me. Pleasing her teachers is what Maria does best—and letting her continue to believe that she had failed in that goal would weaken her self-image. Worse, a seed might be planted that could grow into a strong belief that she is incompetent as a reader. This is too much damage to inflict on one child in one conference. Teachers must always be aware that their acceptance of the student, warts and all, is the essential ingredient for that student's growth.

"Maria, inferring is one of the very hardest things to learn," I told her. "That's why we start on it early in the year and work on it all the time—practice makes perfect! I *expect* everyone to make mistakes on their inferences. Mistakes show me where your thinking is confused so that I can help you learn to straighten out that confused thinking. Every single person in this room is having trouble with inferences. You're learning to think like sophisticated readers—and you're bound to make some mistakes along the way. That's why I'm here. If you could do all this perfectly already, I'd be out of a job!"

Maria smiled shyly—and again looked me straight in the eye. "You are on the right track," I said, smiling back. "Let's talk about where your thinking derailed a bit and see if we can get you on your way. Let's go back to the beginning of this chapter and start looking for the clues the author has left us to trigger an inference."

Maria returned to the first page of the chapter and began reading. In this particular book, Ramona is captivated by the curly hair of a girl named Susan. Cleary describes Susan's hair and Ramona's curiosity about whether those curls would spring back if they were touched. After Maria read this passage, I stopped her.

"In a book," I began, "everything is there for a reason. The author only puts things in a book that will be important later. Beverly Cleary has spent an awful lot of time right here talking about Susan and her curly hair—and how jealous Ramona is of that hair. You've read a Ramona book before. What do you know about Ramona?"

"She gets in lots of trouble doing things she shouldn't."

"Yes, she does. Does she do mean things?"

"No, she is just kind of interested in things and wants to see what will happen."

"You are so right," I said. "So, since she's so interested in Susan's curly hair and wants to see it spring back, what do you think will happen later in the book?"

"She might pull Susan's hair?" Maria guessed.

"*That*," I smiled, "is an inference! Is there any place on this page where it says Ramona is planning to pull Susan's hair?"

"No," Maria responded.

"So, how did you figure that out?"

"I thought about what Ramona usually does and figured that that is why there was so much stuff about Susan's curly hair. It just seems like something Ramona would do."

"See there?" I grinned. "You *do* know how to make inferences! Let's see if we can figure out which column on your chart to put each of those ideas in."

I made sure that Maria understood that one column of her chart was for information the author actually gave us, and one was for what she knew in her head that helped lead her to the third column, which was the inference itself.

"Now, can you see the difference between what you just did and the inferences you made yesterday?"

"I think so," she said, obviously not 100 percent sure.

"Okay, talk me through it," I prompted.

"Yesterday, I just kept putting stuff down that was already in the book. This time I figured something out that wasn't written down already."

"*Bingo!*" I acknowledged. "What a great job you've done today. I'm going to go confer with some other people right now, but I'll check back in with you at the end of reading time to see if you've made another inference on your own. Remember that everything in a book is there for a reason and that part of the fun of reading is figuring out why the author put it there. When you do that, you are inferring."

Several things were done in this conference. The things Maria *did* understand about inferring were affirmed—that inferences always start with the words on the page and join that information to something the reader already knows. The point of the reader's confusion was explicitly named—Maria didn't understand that an inference is something that is never written in the book itself. I was able to guide her thinking as she made an inference on her own by having her discuss what she already knew about the character from reading other Ramona books. I helped her understand that this is one type of prior knowledge on which inferences can be built. Maria then had to show she understood how to use the graphic as a record of her thinking by entering text details, prior knowledge, and inferences on the three-column chart. The conference ended with my asking Maria to explicitly explain what she did differently to make the inference she made with support. It was then made clear she would be trusted to work on her own with this new understanding—but that her work would be checked later on to be sure she understood the day's conference focus. But the entire conference started with my assessment of Maria's response, which had clearly shown her confusion.

Reading Log

Because supported independent reading time is instructional time, students should be held accountable for the way this time is used. Their first task each day is to enter the book they are reading in a reading log.

In my middle school classroom, the students dedicated the first ten pages or so of a spiral notebook to their reading log. The students created columns for the date, the book's title and author, the page on which they started, and the page on which they ended (Figure 10–1). The rest of the notebook was filled with their reading responses.

Because some teachers want to generate a daily grade each week for the pages read during independent reading, a daily reading log can be useful (Figure 10–2). Students who are reading a book at the correct level should be able to read at least ten pages in thirty minutes, so that is the number on which a grade could be based. Students would be expected to read fifty pages a week, with each page worth two points. A student who read only thirty pages that week would receive a 60 for a daily grade. If the logs are copied on both sides of a page, one sheet of

Date	Title & Author	P. Started	P. Finished
10/04	*The Schwa Was Here* by Neal Shusterman	p. 173	p. 189
10/05	Same	p. 204	p. 228 end
10/06	*Walk Two Moons* by Sharon Creech	p. 3	p. 15

Figure 10–1 *A Sample Reading Log*

Name: _____

DAILY READING LOG

Week of _____

Date	Title/Author	Page Started	Page Finished

Total number of pages read: _____

Total number of books finished: _____

Figure 10–2 *Daily Reading Log*

paper is good for two weeks. Running it on brightly colored paper makes it easy to find in students' folders.

These logs should be kept in student reading folders so they are readily available for parent conferences. Since much of what leaves the classroom never finds its way back, I require these logs to be left in the classroom. If the room is in rows, students can pass their folders or notebooks to the front where the teacher can collect them; if the students are in groups, the folders or notebooks can be stacked in the center of the group and picked up there. If the logs and notebooks are lost, valuable assessment information disappears, so it is important to take extremely good care of these treasures.

Assessing Reading Logs

While the students see their reading logs as a way of keeping track of what they're reading and where they are in these texts, these logs are actually invaluable assessment tools for me. By checking their logs, I can identify uncommitted readers who change books every day and begin to work with these students on making better choices. I can look at how many pages are being read and identify students who are making very slow progress and may be in books that are too hard for them. By looking at the pages where they start and end each day, I can see which students are actually reading their books at home, no matter what they may put on their at-home reading assignment. Reading logs tell me which students love fantasy and which prefer realistic fiction. They tell who has read just about every book in a series and will need help moving into other books. And reading logs tell far more about a student's reading level than any one-time assessment ever will.

I regularly analyze each student's reading log, looking for patterns of behavior. I notice:

- If the student is making steady progress through the book—reading about ten pages a day. If not, the book may be too difficult for or uninteresting to him.

- If the student changes books often, abandoning more books than are finished. If so, she has still not learned to choose books well or is still a disengaged reader.

- If the student reads books from the same series over and over again. If so, he has reached a comfort level with the series and will need to be pushed to continue to grow.

- If the student reads in only one genre. If so, she will need to be pushed to try new types of books.

- If the student starts each day at the same place where the reading ended the day before. If so, he is not yet engaged enough in reading to choose to continue reading at home and will need to be shown how to use questions to make reading irresistible.

By taking the time to review each student's reading log regularly, I can often recognize and address problems before they begin to interfere with student learning.

Final Thoughts: The Power of Change

I have not always taught the way I teach now. I have used whole-group texts, handed out copies run from blackline masters, led period-long whole-class discussions of books I chose. I have used independent reading time as a babysitter while I worked with small groups or read a book myself. I taught that way because I believed it was right at the time. My students taught me the error of my ways.

I believe in the power of an independent reading classroom because I have seen it change students' reading lives. You have met some of those students in the pages of this book—but there are so many more. There is the boy who taped a note to the door of my office that read, "Mrs. Allison, could you *please* find me a copy of *Eagle Strike*? I really want to read it and the library is all out." There is the girl who stopped me as I walked through the library and said, "Do you have a copy of *Speak*? Some of my friends are reading it, and I want to read it with them." There are the countless numbers of students who have announced to me or to their teachers, "Miss, this is the first book I ever read all the way through!"

Reading is important—and no matter how much the students in any classroom try to deny it, they are deeply aware of its value. They want to be good readers— and as their teachers we want that for them as well. Independent reading classrooms can help us reach that goal—one day, one student, and one conquered obstacle at a time.

As literacy educators, we need to take a stand. Do we want students to be proficient enough at reading to pass a multiple-choice test—or do we want them to find joy in the written word? Do we want them to think that the only reason to read is to answer someone else's questions—or that reading is a search for their own meanings? By freeing students to choose their own texts and find their own roads through them with our support, we can create lifelong readers. What more important work could there ever be?

STUDY GUIDE

Learning is inherently social. Though sometimes we feel isolated as teachers, most of us know the benefits of taking time to talk with colleagues. It is in these conversations that we find our own ideas clarified and enriched. Develop a professional learning community that works for the culture of your school. Whether you meet once a week or less often; whether you use a professional book as a centerpiece, student writing, or a big, pressing question that concerns your school—make the leap into conversation. While there are many ways to structure a study group, it is most important to foster a climate in which teachers feel free and safe to participate in the ongoing conversations and exchange of ideas. Here are a few things you might consider.

Consider Group Size: You may want to kick off discussion with a general question and then break into smaller groups. Often the optimal number is four or five to ensure there is time for all to exchange ideas. The larger group can reassemble at the end to debrief.

Use Study Questions: Some groups find it more comfortable to start with a few questions to get conversation going. There are various ways to use questions.

- Put three or four questions in an envelope and randomly pull them out for discussion.

- Create a chart with two or three starter questions and ask the group to generate more, tapping their own personal interests and needs.

- Decide on three or four questions and divide the group by interest in the various topics. This allows for a more in-depth study.

- Make copies of the suggested questions for everyone and invite discussion without deciding where to start.

Create an Agenda: Make sure you have planned a beginning and ending time and *always* honor those times. Teachers are busy and knowing there will be a time to start and a time to end is important.

Stay Focused on the Topic: Plan a procedure that is transparent. You might start by saying something like "Let's decide on a signal to use when we feel the discussion is drifting and then have everyone agree to help stay focused."

Include Everyone: Keep groups small enough so that even the quietest member is encouraged to speak. Active listening on everyone's part will help. Remember that periods of silence should be expected when people are thinking.

Share Leadership: Rotate group facilitation. Identify several "duties" for the facilitator. Examples might include a discussion format, suggesting a big idea from a chapter or group of chapters, and synthesizing or summarizing at the end. Remember that in a study group, *everyone* is a learner. This isn't the place for an "expert"!

Create a List of Norms: Simple expectations that are transparent often make study groups function with greater ease and increase potential for success. These can be simple and might include ways to invite a tentative member into the conversation, expectations about listening, start and stop times, and a procedure for refocusing.

Set Dates for the Next Meeting: Always leave knowing when you will meet again and who will facilitate.

Engage in Reflection: Stop from time to time to reflect on what you are learning and how you might make your group's interactions more productive. Make sure you take time to enjoy one another and celebrate your learning.

The following questions relate to the content in each chapter. These are suggestions, and many more concepts and ideas are presented in each chapter. Enjoy!

1 : The Teacher on the Sidelines of Independent Reading

1. Discuss how the nature of today's society works against the idea of students choosing to read for enjoyment. What do you currently do to try to instill a love of reading in the students with whom you work?

2. What is the difference between teaching books and teaching readers? How does this idea change the way you might approach reading instruction in your classroom?

3. What concerns do you have about moving to a classroom where students read in self-selected texts? How can you work together as colleagues to answer these concerns?

4. How have you previously used independent reading in your classroom? How might your presence in deskside conferences during this reading time change the readers in your room?

5. Consider Vygotsky's assertion that growth occurs when students function in their zone of proximal development, an area in which they can be successful only if supported by a "more knowledgeable other." How might that idea shape your thinking about some of the ways your students currently spend their time during your reading class?

6. What is the difference between guidance and support? How would the two look different in a reading classroom?

2 | Planning for Engagement: Coloring and Contouring Students' Expectations

1. Discuss your own student experiences with reading and how they shaped your reading habits. How might students' prior experiences with reading affect their commitment to and progress in your class? What are some specific ways you can help students change their negative attitudes about reading?

2. Discuss the idea of building a concept of *reader*. Are you yourself a reader? What habits define you as such—and how might you share those habits with your students?

3. Book talks are a powerful way to engage students in the classroom. How do you currently use book talks in your classroom? What books do your students find appealing? How can you work together to ensure students are introduced to books that might engage them?

4. McKenna identifies classroom culture as a key component in engaging student readers. What steps can you take to ensure that your classroom culture is centered on reading?

5. Allison recommends having students engage in small-group discussion, even though each of them has been reading a different book. Discuss the implications of this idea. What kinds of discussion prompts could you provide that would lead students to a meaningful discussion of the books they are reading—and how would you assess the quality of those discussions?

3 Clever Matchmaking Between Students and Books

1. Allison stresses the importance of a well-constructed classroom library. Discuss ways to build and maintain a classroom library that will include a wide range of choices including current fiction and nonfiction. How might the availability of these books in your classroom increase the amount of reading your students do?

2. Discuss the idea of the book shopping spree. What specific titles do you think would be most likely to intrigue your students? How might conducting these sprees change the level of engagement in your classroom? How could the information gathered on the record sheets inform your instruction?

3. Allison offers several ideas for making time spent in the school library more productive for students. She specifically stresses helping students understand that their job in the library is to find a book they will understand, finish, and enjoy. Discuss how you currently handle student book choice in the library. How could the idea of finding a book they would finish and enjoy change your students as readers?

4. Many students, particularly those who seem to avoid reading the most, prefer nonfiction texts. This often provides a challenge for teachers who are used to using fiction texts in their classrooms. How familiar are you with quality nonfiction? Collect various titles from your school or classroom libraries or take a trip to a local bookstore to look at the nonfiction titles for adolescents there. How might these books engage your student readers?

4 Direct Instruction and Routines in the Independent Reading Classroom

1. Allison recommends limiting direct instruction to fifteen minutes or less. How would this change the way you plan your lessons? What challenges would this present to you as a teacher? What might be the advantages to students if you made this change?

2. As a group, make a list of five things you plan to teach in the next few weeks in your reading class. Think about how you yourself apply these skills or strategies to your own reading. Choose at least one skill or strategy and together determine the declarative, procedural, and conditional knowledge you will have to provide for your students if they are to be successful in applying this new learning.

3. Allison anchors her lessons in short texts from trade books. Using a stack of fifteen to twenty randomly selected books from your school or classroom libraries, work together to find excerpts you could use to anchor your upcoming lessons. Think aloud as you search for the texts. What specific characteristics must the text you choose have to be a good model for the lesson?

4. Review the ideas presented on creating anchor charts and reading responses. Work together to develop an anchor chart for the skills or strategies you are targeting. Using one of the short texts you have selected, fill in the chart as you would while teaching the lesson. How might this type of response shape students' thinking about the texts they are reading? How might it help them grow as readers?

5. Allison asserts that instruction in an independent reading classroom should be "seamless." Discuss the implications of this statement. What is the relationship between the minilesson, the anchor text, the anchor chart, and the reading response? What kind of planning would such seamless instruction require?

5 Teaching Through Deskside Conferences

1. Discuss the idea of deskside conferences. How might these conferences serve as a tool for differentiating instruction in your classroom?

2. Allison states that deskside conferences are "teacher initiated, but student driven." Discuss the implications of this idea. What unexpected confusions might you uncover during these conferences and how might you respond to them?

3. Keeping meaningful notes on conferences is an important element in an independent reading classroom. What note-taking systems have you tried in the past? What might you try now? What types of notes might you make that would help you know where to go next with your instruction? How might these notes be useful in parent conferences or in discussions with counselors and administrators about individual students?

4. Look back at the lessons you developed based on Chapter 4. What might your conference questions be to assess student understanding of the targeted skills or strategies? What kinds of confusions do you expect to uncover—and how will you redirect confused student thinking?

6 | Capturing the Attention of Our Disengaged Readers

1. Allison asserts that no matter their label there are three types of readers in a classroom: "those who are progressing as expected, those who have fallen behind, and those who are surging ahead." How are you currently meeting the needs of each of these groups of students?

2. Allison prefers the term *delayed reader* to the more common *struggling reader*. How could this change in terminology reflect a difference in teachers' attitudes toward these students?

3. Discuss a delayed reader from your own classroom. How did you identify this student as delayed? What behaviors does he or she exhibit in the classroom? What stands in the way of this student and success? How might deskside conferences accelerate the progress of this student?

4. Think about the on-level readers in your classroom. Do you agree or disagree with the statement that "unless teachers realize that their needs are worthy of focused attention, these readers are in danger of stalling out and failing to make continued progress"? How might this change your teaching?

5. According to Reis and McCoach, a need to conform to their peers coupled with a lack of challenge in the classroom often causes gifted students to become underachievers. How can self-selected reading and deskside conferences be used to reinvigorate and challenge gifted readers?

6. Discuss the sample conferences in the chapter. Focus particularly on Allison's comments. What does she do to draw out the reader's thinking and how does she redirect it when she uncovers a student's confusion?

7 Differentiating Instruction Through Deskside Conferences

1. Discuss the idea that "books that students don't want to read will not help them grow as readers." Do you agree or disagree with this statement? Give specific reasons and examples to support your position.

2. Think about books you have loved and those you have abandoned. What about the books prompted your decision to finish or abandon them? Are your reasons similar to those in Figure 6–1? How would a discussion of this during a minilesson help the readers in your classroom?

3. Allison recommends addressing the issue of distractions in a minilesson. What distracts you while you are reading—and how do you get back into the text after these distractions?

4. Allison details ways to assess the comprehension of disengaged students. Discuss this section of the text. What exactly does Allison do in these conferences that helps these readers understand how to change their approach to the text? Think of a specific student in your class who often seems disengaged from reading. How might this type of conference change that reader?

5. Allison calls questions "the vehicle that drives reading forward." Discuss this idea in detail. Think about what questions you automatically and probably unconsciously generate as you read. How could you share this habit with your students and help them adopt it as well? How could the idea of picking a writer's brain help them understand the difference between simple questions focused on details and richer questions that push the reading forward? How might you address these issues in deskside conferences?

8 Teaching Comprehension in Fiction Texts

1. Discuss the idea that engagement and comprehension are inseparable. How could this idea shape the instruction in your classroom?

2. Most reading teachers are familiar with teaching story structure and character analysis. How do the ideas presented in this chapter fit with how you already approach these ideas in your classroom? What changes might you make based on what you read in this chapter?

3. What confuses the readers in your classroom as they begin to read more sophisticated texts? Using a collection of books from your classroom or school library, look for excerpts that you could use to help your students understand these points of confusion. What key points would you use in your lesson? What declarative, procedural, and conditional knowledge would the students need to have? What questions could you ask in conferences that would uncover these confusions over the way advanced texts are written?

4. Pronouns can be confusing for students both in first-person narratives and in dialogue. From the same collection of books, find excerpts you could use in minilessons to help students understand to whom pronouns refer and how this understanding shapes student understanding. How will you recognize in a conference that pronouns might be the problem?

9 Teaching Comprehension in Nonfiction Texts

1. How do you currently address the challenges of nonfiction texts in your classroom? What steps do you take to be sure students understand how to choose and understand expository texts?

2. Consider the idea that "curiosity is what drives people to read nonfiction." How does this affect your commitment to using nonfiction texts in your classroom? What types of texts might you use? How can you find nonfiction texts that will engage your students?

3. Consider your district and state curriculums. How could nonfiction texts be used to teach required elements in your curriculum? What types of mini-lessons might you provide? What kind of direction might you need to provide in deskside conferences to make students more successful in comprehending these texts?

4. How do you use the K-W-L strategy in your classroom? How could you transfer this knowledge to the reading of informational texts? How would this shape your deskside conferences?

5. Ask your school librarian to provide a list of the most popular books in your school library. How many of them are nonfiction? What are the most popular nonfiction books? How could you use these books in your classroom?

10 Assessing Independent Readers

1. Discuss the true meaning of *assessment*. How do you currently assess the readers in your classroom? How does this assessment inform your instruction?

2. Bring notes from your recent deskside conferences; trade notes with the other members of your study group. What can you tell about the students from the notes their teachers have taken? What direction does instruction need to take to address student needs? How does this inform the instruction in *your* classroom? Discuss the types of comments that best direct instruction in the classroom.

3. Make a list of three to five skills or strategies that you will be teaching in the next few weeks. What graphic organizers might be used as reading responses when these skills or strategies are taught? How will you model their use? How will you use these graphic organizers to assess your students?

4. Bring sample reading logs from your classroom. Work as a group to analyze these logs, looking for what each tells about the reader who completed them. What direction needs to be provided for each of these students so that they can grow? Then look at what these logs can tell you about books your students love. What genres and authors are popular? What specific titles are the students reading and *finishing* the most?

Final Reflection

How might the ideas presented in this book change your instruction in the classroom?

REFERENCES

Professional Books

Agnes, Michael, ed. 2002. *Webster's New World College Dictionary, Fourth Edition*. Cleveland, OH: Wiley Publishing.

Allington, Richard L. 2001. *What Really Matters for Struggling Readers*. New York: Addison-Wesley.

Atwell, Nancie. 2007. *The Reading Zone*. New York: Scholastic.

Aukerman, Maren. 2006. "Who's Afraid of the Big 'Bad Answer'"? *Educational Leadership* 64 (2): 37–41.

Bear, Donald R., Marcia Invernizzi, Shane R. Templeton, and Francine Johnston. 2003. *Words Their Way*. New York: Prentice Hall.

Caine, Renate N., and Geoffrey Caine. 1994. *Making Connections: Teaching and the Human Brain*. Menlo Park, CA: Addison-Wesley.

Calkins, Lucy McCormick. 2001. *The Art of Teaching Reading*. New York: Addison-Wesley.

Carlsen, G. Robert. 1994. "Literature IS . . ." In *Literature IS . . . : Collected Essays by G. Robert Carlsen,* edited by Anne Sherrill and Terry C. Ley, 7–12. Johnson City, TN: Sabre Printers.

Carter, Betty, and Richard F. Abrahamson. 1998. "Castles to Colin Powell: The Truth About Nonfiction." In *Into Focus: Understanding and Creating Middle School Readers*, 313–31. Norwood, MA: Christopher-Gordon.

Carver, Ronald P. 2000. *The Causes of High and Low Reading Achievement*. Mahwah, NJ: Lawrence Erlbaum.

Cassidy, Jack, and Drew Cassidy. 2007. "What's Hot, What's Not for 2007." *Reading Today* 24 (4): 1, 10–11.

Covey, Stephen R. 1989. *The Seven Habits of Highly Effective People*. New York: Simon and Schuster.

Daniels, Harvey. 2002. *Literature Circles: Voice and Choice in Book Clubs and Reading Groups*. Portland, ME: Stenhouse.

Daniels, Harvey, and Marilyn Bizar. 2005. *Teaching the Best Practice Way: Methods That Matter, K–12*. Portland, ME: Stenhouse.

DeLisle, Jim, and Judy Galbraith. 2002. *When Gifted Kids Don't Have All the Answers*. Minneapolis, MN: Free Spirit.

Fountas, Irene C., and Gay Su Pinnell. 2001. *Guiding Readers and Writers, Grades 3–6*. Portsmouth, NH: Heinemann.

Gallagher, Margaret, and P. David Pearson. 1983. "The Instruction of Reading Comprehension." *Contemporary Educational Psychology* 8: 317–44.

Goldman, Daniel. 1995. *Emotional Intelligence*. New York: Bantam.

Guthrie, John T., and Kaeli T. Knowles. 2001. "Promoting Reading Motivation." In *Literacy and Motivation: Reading Engagement in Individuals and Groups,* edited by Ludo Verhoeven and Catherine Snow, 159–76. Mahwah, NJ: Lawrence Erlbaum.

Guthrie, John, and Allan Wigfield. 2000. "Engagement and Motivation in Reading." In *Handbook of Reading Research,* Volume 3, edited by Michael L. Kamil, Peter B. Mosenthal, P. David Pearson, and Rebecca Barr, 403–22. Mahwah, NJ: Lawrence Erlbaum.

Harste, Jerome C., and Christine Leland. 2007. "On Getting Lost, Finding One's Direction, and Teacher Research." *Voices from the Middle* 14 (3): 7–11.

Harvey, Stephanie, and Anne Goudvis. 2007. *Strategies That Work: Teaching Comprehension to Enhance Understanding*. York, ME: Stenhouse.

Jobe, Ron, and Mary Dayton-Sakari. 1999. *Reluctant Readers*. Markham, ON: Pembroke.

Keene, Ellin Oliver, and Susan Zimmermann. 2007. *Mosaic of Thought: The Power of Comprehension Strategy Instruction*. Portsmouth, NH: Heinemann.

Krashen, Stephen D. 2004. *The Power of Reading: Insights from Research*. Portsmouth, NH: Heinemann.

Langer, Judith A. 1995. *Envisioning Literature*. New York: Teachers College Press.

Lesesne, Teri S. 2003. *Making the Match: The Right Book for the Right Reader at the Right Time, Grades 4–12*. Portland, ME: Stenhouse.

———. 2006. *Naked Reading: Uncovering What Tweens Need to Become Lifelong Readers*. Portland, ME: Stenhouse.

Lyons, Carol A. 2003. *Teaching Struggling Readers*. Portsmouth, NH: Heinemann.

McKenna, Michael C. 2001. "Development of Reading Attitudes." In *Literacy and Motivation*, edited by Ludo Verhoeven and Catherine Snow, 135–58. Mahwah, NJ: Lawrence Erlbaum.

Neuman, Susan B., and David K. Dickson. 2006. *Handbook of Early Literacy Research*. New York: Guilford Press.

Ogle, Donna. 1986. "K-W-L: A Teaching Model That Develops Active Reading in Expository Text." *The Reading Teacher* 39 (6): 564–70.

Raphael, Taffy E., Laura S. Pardo, and Kathy Highfield. 2002. *Book Club: A Literature-Based Curriculum*. Lawrence, MA: Small Planet.

Reeves, Anne R. 2004. *Adolescents Talk About Reading: Exploring Resistance to and Engagement with Text*. Newark, DE: International Reading Association.

Reis, Sally M., and D. Betsy McCoach. 2002. "Underachievement in Gifted Students." In *The Social and Emotional Development of Gifted Children: What Do We Know?* edited by Maureen Neihart, Sally M. Reis, Nancy M. Robinson, and Sidney M. Moon, 81–91. Washington, DC: National Association for Gifted Children.

Rosenblatt, Louise M. 1965. *Literature as Exploration*. New York: Modern Language Association.

———. 1978. *The Reader, the Text, the Poem*. Carbondale, IL: Southern Illinois University Press.

———. 2005. *Making Meaning with Texts*. Portsmouth, NH: Heinemann.

Sibberson, Franki, and Karen Szymusiak. 2003. *Still Learning to Read: Teaching Students in Grades 3–6*. Portland, ME: Stenhouse.

Tomlinson, Carol. 1999. *The Differentiated Classroom: Responding to the Needs of All Learners*. Alexandria, VA: Association for Supervision and Curriculum Development.

Vygotsky, Lev S. 1978. *Mind in Society: The Development of Higher Psychological Processes*. Cambridge, MA: Harvard University Press.

———. 1986. *Thought and Language*. Cambridge, MA: MIT Press.

Winebrenner, Susan. 2001. *Teaching Gifted Kids in the Regular Classroom*. Minneapolis, MN: Free Spirit.

Presentations

Hoyt, L. 2008. Presentation to Spring Branch ISD language arts school improvement specialists. Houston, Texas.

Trade Books

Anderson, Laurie Halse. 2006. *Speak*. New York: Puffin.

Avi. 2005. *The Book Without Words*. New York: Hyperion.

Balliet, Blue. 2004. *Chasing Vermeer*. New York: Scholastic.

Bledsoe, Glen, and Karen E. 2002. *The World's Fastest Truck (Built for Speed)*. Mankato, MN: Capstone.

Bloom, Becky. 1999. *Wolf!* New York: Scholastic.

Brokaw, Tom. 2007. *Boom! Voices of the Sixties*. New York: Random House.

Bruchac, Joseph. 2001. *Skeleton Man*. New York: HarperCollins.

Cabot, Meg. Princess Diaries series. New York: Harper Trophy.

Carter, Alden R. 2001. "Satyagraha." In *On the Fringe,* edited by Don Gallo, 165–80. New York: Dial.

Cooney, Caroline B. 1990. *The Face on the Milk Carton*. New York: Bantam.

———. 1997. *The Terrorist*. New York: Scholastic.

DiCamillo, Kate. 2000. *Because of Winn-Dixie*. Cambridge, MA: Candlewick Press.

———. 2002. *The Tiger Rising*. New York: Candlewick Press.

Draper, Sharon M. 1994. *Tears of a Tiger*. New York: Aladdin.

du Maurier, Daphne. 1971. *Rebecca*. New York: Avon.

Finchler, Judy. 2006. *Miss Malarky Leaves No Reader Behind*. New York: Walker Books for Young Readers.

Franzen, Jonathan. 2002. *The Corrections*. New York: Picador.

Glenday, Craig, ed. 2008. *Guinness: World Records 2008*. New York: Guinness World Records Ltd.

Haddix, Margaret P. 1998. *Among the Hidden*. New York: Aladdin.

Hahn, Mary Downing. 1986. *Wait Till Helen Comes: A Ghost Story*. New York: Avon.

Hansen, Ole Steen. 2005. *The AH-64 Apache Helicopter: Cross-Sections*. Kentwood, LA: Edge Books.

Hinton, S. E. 1967. *The Outsiders*. New York: Puffin.

Horowitz, Anthony. 2001. *Point Blank*. New York: Penguin.

———. 2003. *Eagle Strike*. New York: Philomel.

Hughes, Monica. Creepy Creatures series. Orlando, FL: Raintree.

Kline, Suzy. Herbie Jones series. New York: Puffin.

Korman, Gordon. 2000. *No More Dead Dogs*. New York: Hyperion.

———. Island, Dive, Everest, and Kidnapped series. New York: Scholastic.

———. On the Run series. New York: Scholastic.

Lubar, David. 2005. *Invasion of the Road Weenies: And Other Warped and Creepy Tales*. New York: Starscape.

———. 2005. *Sleeping Freshmen Never Lie*. New York: Penguin.

Lyon, George Ella. 1998. *A Sign*. New York: Orchard.

———. 1999. *Book*. New York: DK Children.

Martínez, Ruben. 2004. *The New Americans*. New York: The New Press.

Masoff, Joy. 2000. *Oh, Yuck! The Encyclopedia of Everything Nasty*. New York: Workman.

———. 2006. *Oh, Yikes! History's Grossest Moments*. New York: Workman.

McDonald, Megan. Judy Moody series. New York: Candlewick.

McPhail, David. 1997. *Edward and the Pirates*. New York: Little, Brown.

Nixon, Joan Lowery. 1991. *Whispers from the Dead*. New York: Laurel Leaf.

O'Farrell, Maggie. 2006. *The Vanishing Act of Esme Lennox*. Orlando, FL: Harcourt.

Oxlade, Chris, Paul Mason, and Holly Wallace. Can Science Solve? series. Chicago, IL: Heinemann Library.

Padgett, Marty. 2005. *Hot Cars Cool Rides*. Orlando, FL: Tangerine Press.

Park, Barbara. Junie B. Jones series. New York: Random House.

Pearson, Mary E. 2008. *The Adoration of Jenna Fox*. New York: Henry Holt.

Philbrick, Nathaniel. 2006. *Mayflower*. New York: Penguin.

Quindlen, Anna. 1998. *How Reading Changed My Life*. New York: Ballantine.

Rowling, J. K. Harry Potter series. New York: Scholastic.

Ryan, Pam Muñoz. 2000. *Esperanza Rising*. New York: Scholastic.

Sachar, Louis. 1987. *There's a Boy in the Girls' Bathroom*. New York: Dell Yearling.

———. 1998. *Holes*. New York: Dell Yearling.

Schraff, Anne. 2002. *Someone to Love Me*. West Berlin, NJ: Townsend Press.

Shan, Darren. Cirque du Freak series. New York: Little, Brown.

———. 2000. *A Living Nightmare*. Book 1 in The Saga of Darren Shan. New York: Little, Brown.

Shusterman, Neal. 2006. *Everlost*. New York: Simon and Schuster Books for Young Readers.

Sleator, William. 1999. *Rewind*. New York: Penguin.

———. 2005. *The Last Universe*. New York: Harry N. Abrams.

Spinelli, Jerry. 1990. *Maniac Magee*. New York: Little, Brown.

———. 2000. *Stargirl*. New York: Alfred A. Knopf.

———. 2007. *Eggs*. New York: Little, Brown.

Steinbeck, John. 1981. *Of Mice and Men*. New York: Bantam.

Stilton, Geronimo. 2004. *Geronimo Stilton No. 9: A Fabumouse Vacation for Geronimo*. New York: Scholastic.

Stine, R. L. Goosebumps series. New York: Scholastic.

Twain, Mark. 1981. *Huckleberry Finn*. New York: Bantam.

Van Draanen, Wendy. 2001. *Flipped*. New York: Scholastic.

Walsh, Ann. 2007. *Horse Power*. Custer, WA: Orca Book.

Weir, Alison. 1999. *The Life of Elizabeth I*. New York: Ballantine.

Woodson, Jacqueline. 2001. *The Other Side*. New York: G. P. Putnam's Sons.

Wright, Betty Ren. 1983. *The Dollhouse Murders*. New York: Scholastic.

———. 1991. *A Ghost in the House*. New York: Scholastic.

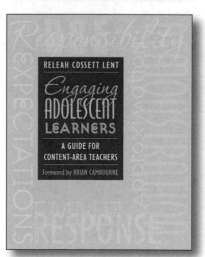